Who When Where?

Who? When? Where?

The Story of the Guinness Lithographs

Emma Mason

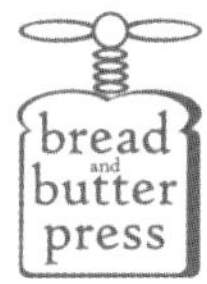 bread and butter press

Published by Bread and Butter Press
3 Cornfield Terrace
Eastbourne
East Sussex
BN21 4NN
www.breadandbutterpress.co.uk

ISBN 978-0-9955037-1-7

Printed in England by Northend Creative Print Solutions, Sheffield

Cover illustration detail from Barnett Freedman 'The Darts Champion'

Contents

Acknowledgements

I would like to give special thanks to all the artists and their families who have been so supportive. I would also like to thank Craig Glenday, Jenny Heller and the team at Guinness World Records, Simon Lawrence at Fleece Press, Simon Martin at Pallant House Gallery, Jeremy Parrett at Manchester Metropolitan University, Dr Patrick Chaplin, Darts Historian, Guinness Breweries and Northend Creative Print Solutions.

Preface

I first came across the Guinness series of lithographs when I saw a few of the prints at an auction. The prints had the title *A Guinness Lithograph* along the bottom of the image, I knew nothing about them but I recognised the names of several of the artists. Intrigued, and, after some initial research, I found that they were part of a series of lithographs produced for Guinness Breweries but that little else was known about them. This was odd as the images were by important artists of the time and the lack of information was in contrast to that available about other series of lithographs produced in post-war Britain; The School Prints Series, The Coronation Series and The Lyons Lithographs.

I decided to research the lithographs more fully and to collect all the prints known to be in the series. It took me several years but eventually I found all the lithographs known to exist. The next step was to discover the story behind the lithographs. I soon discovered both a wonderful story and a remarkable series of lithographs.

Emma Mason

'Officially Amazing!'

Guinness has always been a visual brand. With its distinctive black and white 20-oz 'imperial' pint glass and the golden harp logo, the product is a powerful visual in its own right. Add to this memorable icons such as the toucan (with thanks to crime writer Dorothy L Sayers for her accompanying "Guinness is good for you" slogan) and the myriad comical images you'll find in this visual history and it's clear to see why the love-it-or-hate-it stout has earned respect for its iconic status, if not for its creamy, bitter taste.

So too has the visual been central to *The Guinness Book of Records* or *Guinness World Records,* as it's been known since 1999. (Diageo sold the rights in 1999 to Gullane Children's Books, publishers of Thomas The Tank Engine.) The very first record to be found in the first edition, published in 1955, is that of the highest mountain in the world, Everest, which appears in all its glory on the book's full-colour frontispiece. And peppered throughout the 198 page book are 16 monochrome plates with photographs and illustrations of record holders as diverse as the largest building (the Pentagon), the most expensive football player (Hans Jeppson) and the fastest aircraft (the Bell XI-A). The founding editors, Ross and Norris McWhirter clearly understood the power of the visual, resorting to painting vivid pictures with their words whenever it wasn't possible to show a photo or artwork.

The history of Guinness stout advertising is well documented, but what's rarely mentioned is the context for such effective campaigns. Yes, the idea has always been to sell more beer but Guinness' unique circumstances – a brewer selling their product in a rival brewer's pub – put extra pressure on the brewery to compete. To stand out Guinness resorted to compelling slogans and powerful visuals, and the result is a rich history of innovative, creative campaigns.

Just as Guinness had to battle the competition from rival brewers, so too has the *Guinness World Records* book had to face up to ever-more-engaging demands for readers' time, particularly from the Internet and video gaming. For us, it's the visual that's the key to hooking in new readers. We're not ashamed to say that we use every trick in the book to make reading a pleasurable experience for younger readers, with features such as 3D glasses, glow-in-the-dark pages, fold-out features and, most recently, augmented reality all being employed at various times over the years to keep kids interested. I consider this merely an extension of Sir Hugh's original intention of revealing to the world just how amazing this superlative material is.

I hope you enjoy discovering these lithographs – they are, as we would say at *Guinness World Records,* Officially Amazing!

Craig Glenday
Editor-in-Chief, Guinness World Records

Foreword

In the past, modern art was often perceived as something only to be enjoyed by 'in-the-know' collectors in elitist galleries. This perception has of course changed dramatically in recent years, with more people now going to museums and galleries than to football matches, and the experience of going to public exhibitions now enjoyed by a cross section of society. The story of how modern art has touched the lives of ordinary people in the twentieth-century is fascinating: whether through groups of artists such as the Ashington coal miners in the 1930s, or the billboards in London painted by artists protesting during the Spanish Civil War, the War Artists Scheme in the Second World War engaging artists such as Henry Moore to record the experiences of people sheltering from the Blitz, or indeed the innovative print schemes that were aimed at introducing modern art to audiences that might never step into an art gallery.

In 2007, Pallant House Gallery held an exhibition of The School Prints, a series of lithographs by artists such as LS Lowry, Pablo Picasso, Henri Matisse and Julian Trevelyan, which brought original modern art into the classrooms of the 1940s and 50s. It was one of a number of enterprising schemes that also memorably included The Contemporary Lithographs in the 1930s and The Lyons Lithographs for teahouses in the 1940s. But despite the worldwide fame of *The Guinness Book of Records* and the Irish brewery from which it originally took its name, the story of how The Guinness Lithographs brought modern art into public houses across Britain has never been properly told.

Emma Mason must be congratulated bringing together this wonderful group of prints and for piecing together this fascinating lost social and artistic history for the art lovers of today in this beautiful book. It is a great pleasure for us to be showing these at Pallant House Gallery in the context of our collection of Modern British art.

Simon Martin
Artistic Director
Pallant House Gallery

'Wherever people congregate to talk, they will argue, and sometimes the joy lies in the arguing and would be lost if there were any definite answer. But more often the argument takes place on a dispute of fact, and it can be very exasperating if there is no immediate means of settling the argument. Who was the first to swim the channel? Where is England's deepest well, or Scotland's highest tree, or Ireland's oldest church? How many died in history's worst rail crash? Who gained the biggest majority in parliament? What is the highest point in our country? And so on. How much heat these innocent questions can raise! Guinness, in producing this book, hopes that it may assist in resolving many such disputes, and may, we hope, turn heat into light.'

Chairman of Arthur Guinness & Co, the Rt Hon the Earl of Iveagh
September 1955

The Lithographs

The Guinness Lithographs consist of twelve prints made in two series, one series in 1956 and the other a few years later in 1962. The artists in each are as follows:

Artists for Series 1	Artists for Series 2
Edward Ardizzone	David Gentleman
Bernard Cheese	Alistair Grant
Barnett Freedman	Richard Guyatt
Ronald Glendening	Leonard Rosoman
Edwin La Dell	Rosamund Steed
Brian Robb	Carel Weight

The Story of the Guinness Lithographs

Before we can begin the story of The Guinness Lithographs we should first give some background to the Guinness Breweries who commissioned the series. Guinness Breweries started in 1759 when the first Arthur Guinness acquired a brewery in Dublin. It was here some years later that the brewery started to brew a dark beer called porter. After some changes, making the beer stronger, it became known as Guinness, the drink we know today. Throughout the nineteenth-century the popularity of Guinness grew and Guinness Breweries became one of the most successful and established breweries in the UK. By the 1950s, the time when the first lithographs were made, Guinness was one of the most popular stouts on the market despite competition from other breweries. At the time the managing director of Guinness Breweries was Sir Hugh Beaver and it is because of him that The Guinness Lithographs came about.

The story of the lithographs begins in November 1951 when Sir Hugh Beaver was with a shooting party in the North Slob, by the River Slaney in County Wexford, Ireland. He became involved in an argument about which was the fastest game bird in Europe, the koshin golden plover or the grouse? That evening he realised that it was impossible to confirm from reference books whether or not the golden plover was Europe's fastest game bird. Beaver knew that there must be numerous other questions debated nightly in pubs throughout Britain and Ireland, but there was no book in the world with which to settle such arguments. It occurred to him that a book supplying the answers to these sort of questions might prove popular.

From this unusual beginning Guinness Breweries set about creating such a book, which was to be called *The Guinness Book of Records*. In August 1954, after a boardroom lunch at Park Royal, they commissioned 'fact-finding agency' McWhirter Twins Limited to compile the first book. The agency was run by twin brothers, Norris (1925-2004), and Ross (1925-75) McWhirter, who had set up their business to provide facts and figures to newspapers, yearbooks, encyclopaedias and advertisers.

Norris McWhirter wrote an article called 'The Story behind *The Guinness Book of Records*' for the company magazine *Guinness Time* in the Christmas edition of 1955. He described how they set out on fact finding for the first book:

'Letters began to pour forth addressed to astrophysicists, physiologists, zoologists, meteorologists, vulcanologists, botanists, ornithologists, microlepidopterists, concologists, virologists, economists, numismatists, criminologists, etimologists, incunabulists, campinologists, gemmologists, metrologists, pryphologists, toxicologists, spelæologists, malocologists, herpetologists, hagiologists, horologists, mycologists and gerontologists. Life became a battle of extracting the '-ests' from the '-ists'. Aided by tape recorders and electric typewriters, the output touched 160 letters a week.' 1.

Guinness set up a publishing subsidiary to take on the task of producing the book and a small office was set up in Fleet Street. In June 1955 after only a little more than three months of intensive work collecting data, including weekends, the McWhirters and their team had finished the book. In late summer 1955 an advance copy of the first Book of Records was sent to the Sussex home of Sir Hugh Beaver. He was delighted with the: *'speed of which the spirit of his idea had been turned into substance.' 2.*

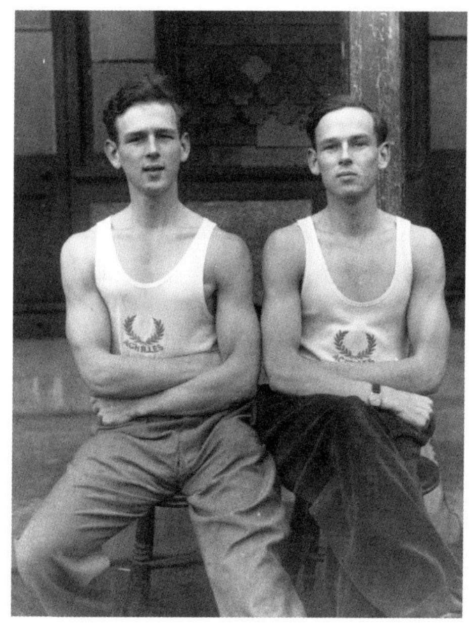

Twin Athletes
The McWhirters pictured in 1953
Photo by Mrs Dulce R Stuart/D R Stuart
Getty Images.

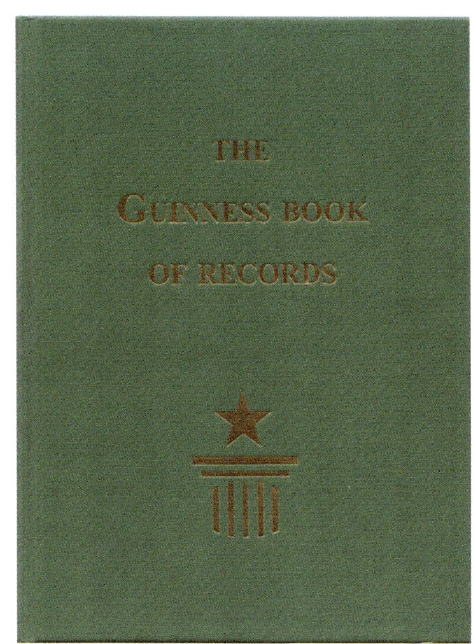

The first *Guinness Book of Records*, 1955.

The first edition had an emerald green cover, was 7 inches wide, 10 inches long and stretched to 198 pages. The foreword to the book was written by the then Chairman of Arthur Guinness & Co, the Rt Hon the Earl of Iveagh and in it he sums up the motivations behind the book perfectly:

'Wherever people congregate to talk, they will argue, and sometimes the joy lies in the arguing and would be lost if there were any definite answer. But more often the argument takes place on a dispute of fact, and it can be very exasperating if there is no immediate means of settling the argument. Who was the first to swim the channel? Where is England's deepest well, or Scotland's highest tree, or Ireland's oldest church? How many died in history's worst rail crash? Who gained the biggest majority in parliament? What is the highest point in our country? And so on. How much heat these innocent questions can raise! Guinness, in producing this book, hopes that it may assist in resolving many such disputes, and may, we hope, turn heat into light.' 3.

In early October 1955 the book was ready for distribution. The first edition of the book was for 50,000 copies. That Autumn the brewery announced news of the new book in their staff newsletter *Guinness Time* explaining that one copy of the book was to be set aside for each member of the brewery and available to them at 2/6 (two shillings and six pence), half the retail price. Other copies could then be purchased through booksellers at the retail price of five shillings.

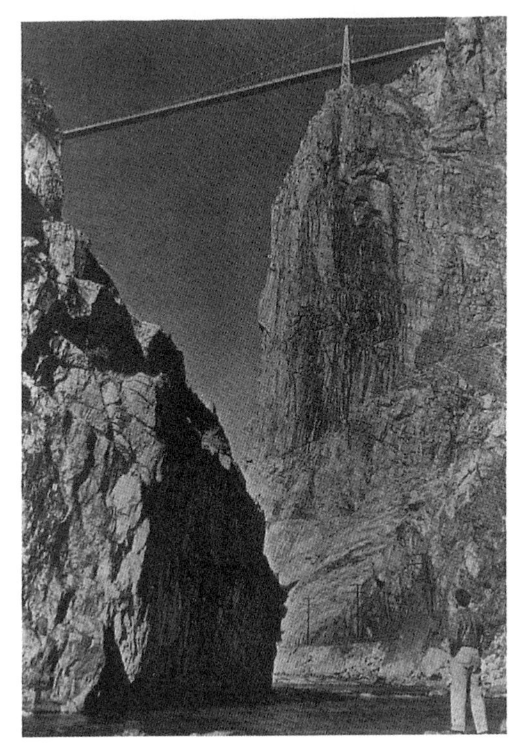

Where is
the
highest
Suspension
Bridge
in the
World?

Find the answer in
"The Guinness Book of Records"

Image from *Guinness Time,* Autumn issue 1955.

Image from *Guinness Time, Christmas issue 1962.*

It was the first time anything of its kind had ever been printed and no one had any idea what a global phenomenon it was about to become. Demand for the book outpaced production in the first five months from October 1955 to February 1956 when the book was declared 'out of print' after sales of 140,000 books. The book went to the top of the British best-seller list by Christmas and in September 1956 it was launched in the US under the title, *Guinness Superlatives,* to great success.

The rest, as they say, is history. The *Guinness Book of Records* has become an annual fixture, printed each year in the Autumn to coincide with Christmas sales and still tops the best-seller lists, now under the title *Guinness World Records*.

The first book was to be available in pubs and canteens across the UK and with the success of the initial launch Guinness Breweries decided to publicise the book with images for the walls of the pubs and canteens, large images for all to see. The ideal medium was print, and in particular lithography and these publicity images became known as The Guinness Lithographs. This is the story of the lithographs.

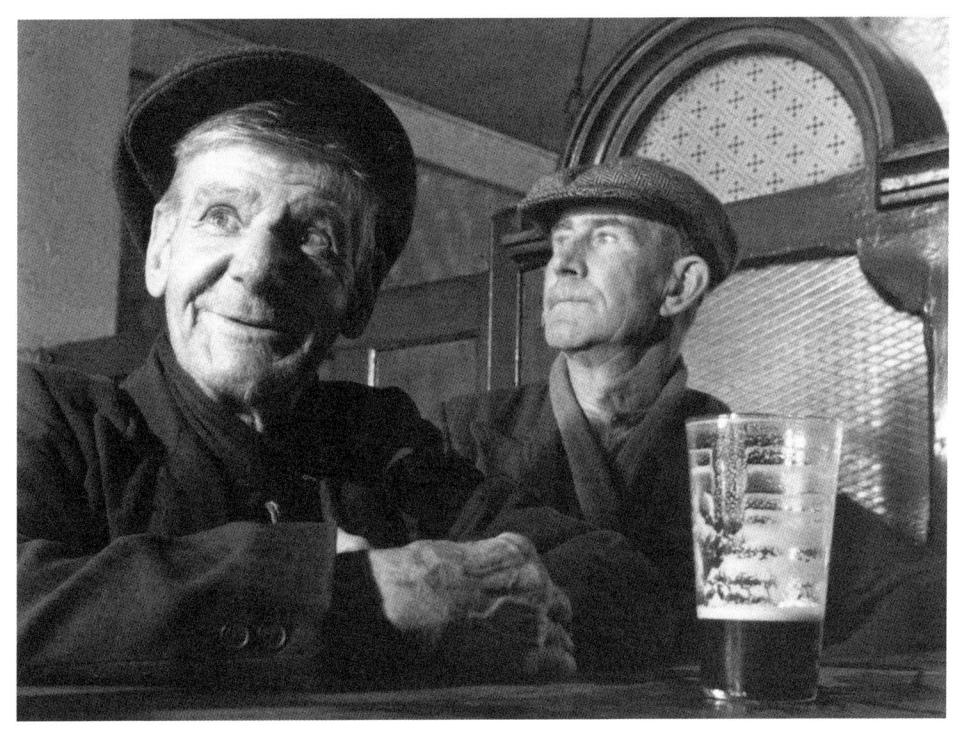

A Dublin Pint

Henry Barter with a pint of Guinness at John Mullet's bar in Amiens Street, Dublin, 22nd August 1953.

Photo by Bert Hardy/Stringer Picture Post/ Getty Images.

A Pint, a Print and a Book

'My company are planning to distribute a number of auto-lithographs to public houses, working men's clubs, works canteens etc. The subjects of these lithographs are to be taken from the Guinness Book of Records. *This book, which has been published in very large quantities, is a collection of facts which give the superlatives in many different fields, covering such items as sporting events, human achievements, the world structures etc, etc. We would very much like to commission you to produce one of these auto-lithographs.'* 4.

This was written in April 1956 by Tommy Marks of Arthur Guinness Breweries and sent to a number of artists of the day who were familiar with lithography. Tommy Marks joined Guinness in 1955 as the advertising manager. He was to become a very important part of the team, known affectionately as TLM. He later became a director in the company, receiving an OBE for his work. He died in 1971 and the Autumn issue of the company magazine paid tribute in the article, *A man of imagination & understanding:*

'He added a certain visual distinction and clarity to all the work he handled. He was not in any conventional sense an artist and would have recoiled from the word artistic, but he was a man of many talents, possessed of a quiet and positive understanding of the arts and the knack of winning friendship and respect of artists of many sorts.' 5.

During his time at Guinness, Marks, in addition to overseeing the lithographs, also initiated the Guinness Poetry Awards and five *Guinness Books of Poetry* were produced.

With his interest in the arts and his creative outlook Tommy Marks was greatly suited to overseeing the lithograph project. His letter, sent out to selected artists inviting them to take part in The Guinness Lithographs, marked the start of the commission as a real life project but discussions about it had been going on for some time before this point. Marks had discussed the project in detail with the artist Barnett Freedman, the man that Guinness employed to advise them on the lithographs.

Barnett Freedman (1901-58) was an artist and designer with an excellent reputation in the arts. He was the perfect man for the job, known as a master of lithography. Freedman had studied at St Martins School of Art and at The Royal College of Art (RCA) and he had also learnt the skills of lithography under a technical apprenticeship at commercial printers, the Baynard Press:

'Freedman was somewhat unusual in this dual training and was one of only a relatively small number of artists who received a formal fine art education as well as a more practical art-based apprenticeship under a professional printer.' 6.

Having both academic fine art training and a practical apprenticeship gave Freedman a very clear understanding of lithography. He was able to use this experience both in his teaching and in his role advising on commissions. A few years before working with Guinness, Freedman had been the advisor on a series of prints known as The Lyons Lithographs (1946-55) made for display in the Lyons Teahouses. This ambitious project produced forty lithographs at a time of widespread austerity in post-war Britain. It was quite an achievement and much of the success was due to Barnett Freedman.

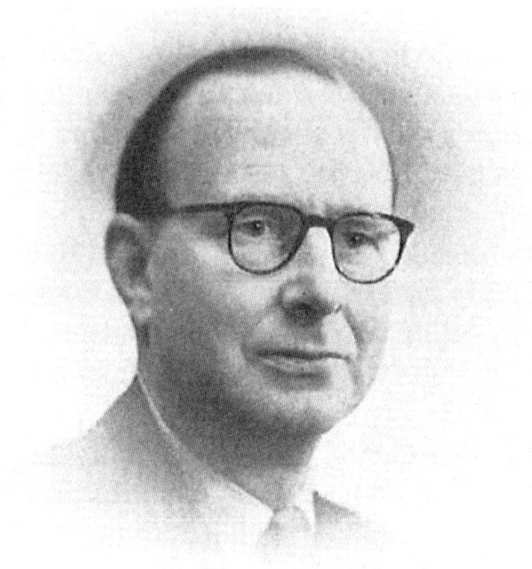

Tommy Marks. Image courtesy of Guinness Archive at Guinness Storehouse in Dublin.

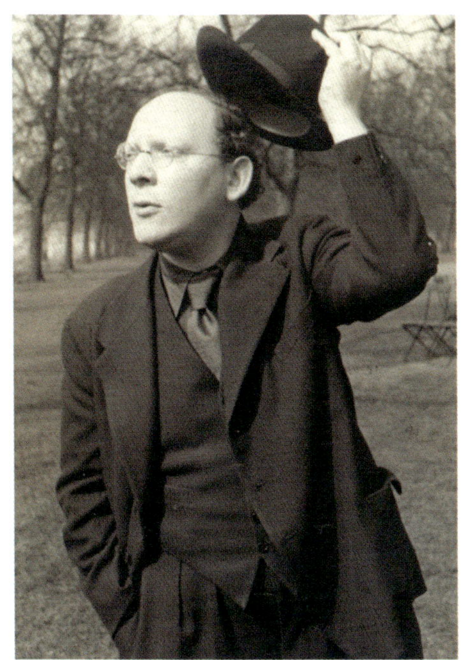

Barnett Freedman. Image courtesy of Manchester Metropolitan University Special Collections.

With The Lyons Lithograph series complete Freedman was ready for a new project. Throughout the previous year Freedman had been working as an advisor to Guinness, a role that was initially described by Marks as 'somewhat nebulous'. The role involved Freedman inviting people from the world of 'Art and Letters' to act as advisors over relations between Guinness and the public. Guinness saw artists as being in touch with public opinion and taste. The advisory role that Freedman was invited to take on was outlined by Marks in a letter to him written in November 1955:

'Dear Barnett,
You will remember that when we met a few weeks ago I outlined to you a scheme whereby we were proposing to invite certain people from the world of Art and Letters to act as advisors to us over the whole field of our relations with the public.' 7.

Tommy Marks explains the role to Freedman more in his letter asking him to:

'...take an interest in our affairs and proffer us your advice for a period say of 12 months commencing 1st January 1956. I do not think the duties will be very arduous – we should like you to visit our brewery occasionally and to dine with us in London once a month, when we could have a general discussion on any ideas you may care to put forward.' 8.

For this advisory role Freedman would receive a total of five hundred guineas, paid in equal parts over a year. Guinness emphasised to Freedman that they did not require him to confine his ideas to the narrow field of advertising but would like ideas and discussions to range over the whole of Guinness's relations with the public. This was a very forward thinking view for a large company in the mid 1950s and it shows that they were aware of the need to engage with their audience. Guinness recognised the positive benefits of understanding their audience and of being seen as a company that supported their public.

ARTHUR GUINNESS SON & CO. (PARK ROYAL) LTD.

ARTHUR GUINNESS SON & CO. (PARK ROYAL) LTD.

TELEPHONE:
ELGAR 7700

PARK ROYAL BREWERY
LONDON, N.W.10

TELEGRAMS:
"GUINNESS, HARLES,
LONDON"

OUR REFERENCE
TLM/M

Please reply to ADVERTISING DEPARTMENT

YOUR REFERENCE

2nd November, 1955

Barnett Freedman Esq., C.B.E.,
59, Cornwall Gardens,
London, S.W.7.

Please return to me.

Dear Barnett,

 You will remember that when we met a few weeks ago I outlined to you a scheme whereby we were proposing to invite certain people from the world of Art and Letters to act as advisors to us over the whole field of our relations with the public.

 This scheme was, and to some extent still is, somewhat nebulous, but we feel that we should benefit from suggestions put forward by people who, by reason of their own vocation, are in touch with public opinion and taste.

 I am, therefore, inviting you to take an interest in our affairs and proffer us your advice for a period say of 12 months commencing 1st January 1956. I do not think the duties will be very arduous - we should like you to visit our Brewery occasionally and to dine with us in London once a month, when we could have a general discussion on any ideas you might care to put forward. Should these ideas involve the actual exercise of your art - by that I mean designing or painting - and should we decide to go ahead with the proposal we should, of course, be at liberty to do so without necessarily coming to you for the work. In fact, we should like to feel that if desired we could consult you as to where to go. However, should we decide to ask you to undertake the work for us, then naturally we should expect to pay for this over and above any consultative fee, which I will mention later in this letter.

 I do not want you to think that such ideas as we are seeking are to be confined to the narrow field of advertising. We would wish them to range over the whole of our relations with the public. If you would like to undertake this task for us for a period of a year, we should be prepared to pay you five hundred guineas in equal quarterly payments.

 I should be most grateful if you would let me have your decision as soon as possible.

 Kind regards,

 Yours sincerely,

 Tommy Marks

 T.L. Marks.

By publishing a series of prints Guinness were following in the footsteps of the J Lyons & Co who had produced The Lyons Series of lithographs (1946-55), which were placed on the walls of their teahouses. The Lyons lithographs were described as:

'...offering demonstrable support for British artists and, in turn, they were consciously establishing Lyons as a corporate patron of the visual arts.' 9.

This was just as applicable to Guinness and being viewed as a patron of the visual arts was important to the company. This comes across in the letters between Guinness and Freedman and in the fact Freedman was employed in his advisory role.

Freedman agreed to take on the role and on 1st December 1955 he went for lunch at the Guinness Brewery in Park Royal where he met members of the board. Freedman then started officially as advisor on 1st January 1956. By this time sales of the *Guinness Book of Records* were exceeding all expectations.

Letter from Tommy Marks to Barnett Freedman
Courtesy of Manchester Metropolitan University
Special Collections.

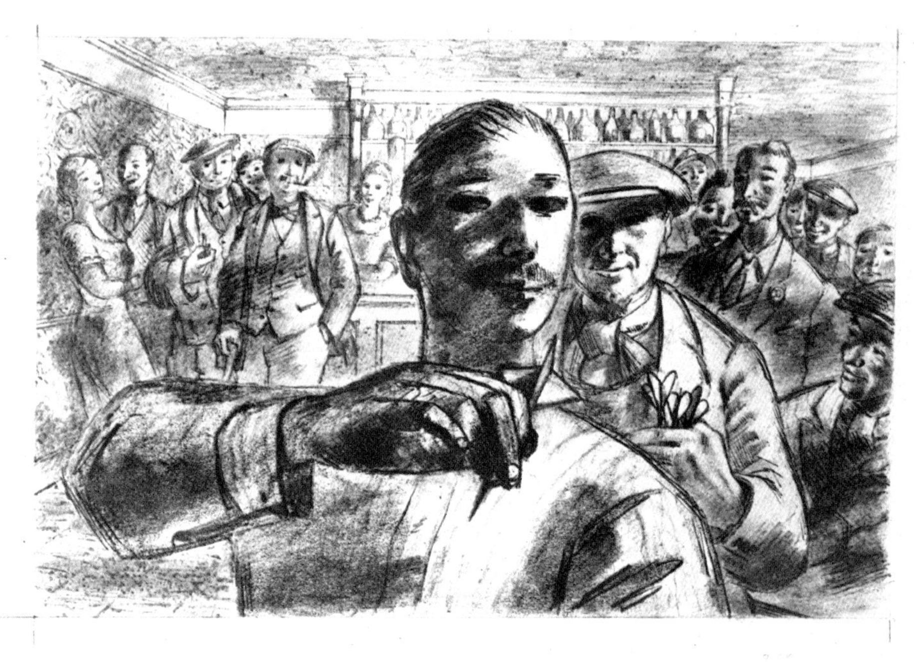

The Darts Champion sketch by Barnett Freedman
Courtesy of Manchester Metropolitan University
Special Collections.

26

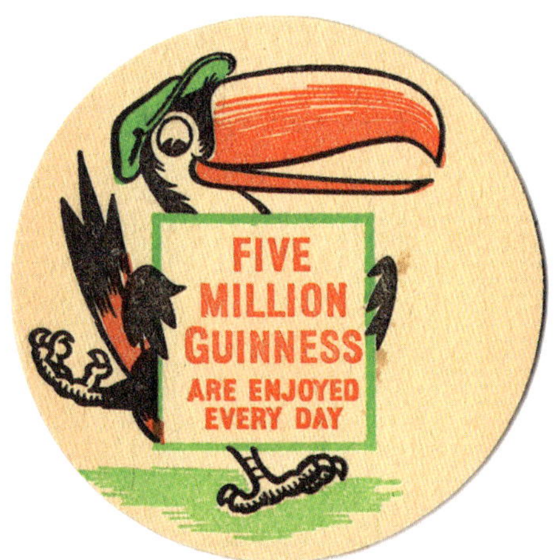

During 1956 the project for The Guinness Lithographs became a reality. Freedman not only oversaw the project but he was also one of the artists to make a lithograph for the series with his image of *The Darts Champion*.

The timing for such a print-based project was very good with the post-war years proving to be exciting times for those involved in print. There were exhibitions with new galleries supporting printmakers, such as the St George's Gallery, which opened in Cork Street, London in 1955 by Robert Erskine:

'The pioneer in what has sometimes been called the post-war print renaissance was the Hon. Robert Erskine, who began a publishing programme at the St George's Gallery, London, in the second half of the 1950s. He was inspired by various European houses such as the Guild de la Gravure, and said he wanted good art to reach the "mums and dads of Pinner and Wigan". 10.

The St George's Gallery was to provide a specialist outlet for the new and growing number of printmakers, many of them working in lithography. There was also a renewed interest in commissioning printmakers and sponsorship of print publishing flourished.

The 1950s was a busy time for artists and these types of commissions were not uncommon. In the post-war years there was a new optimism and people were keen to brighten up public spaces. Various commercial organisations had commissioned artists

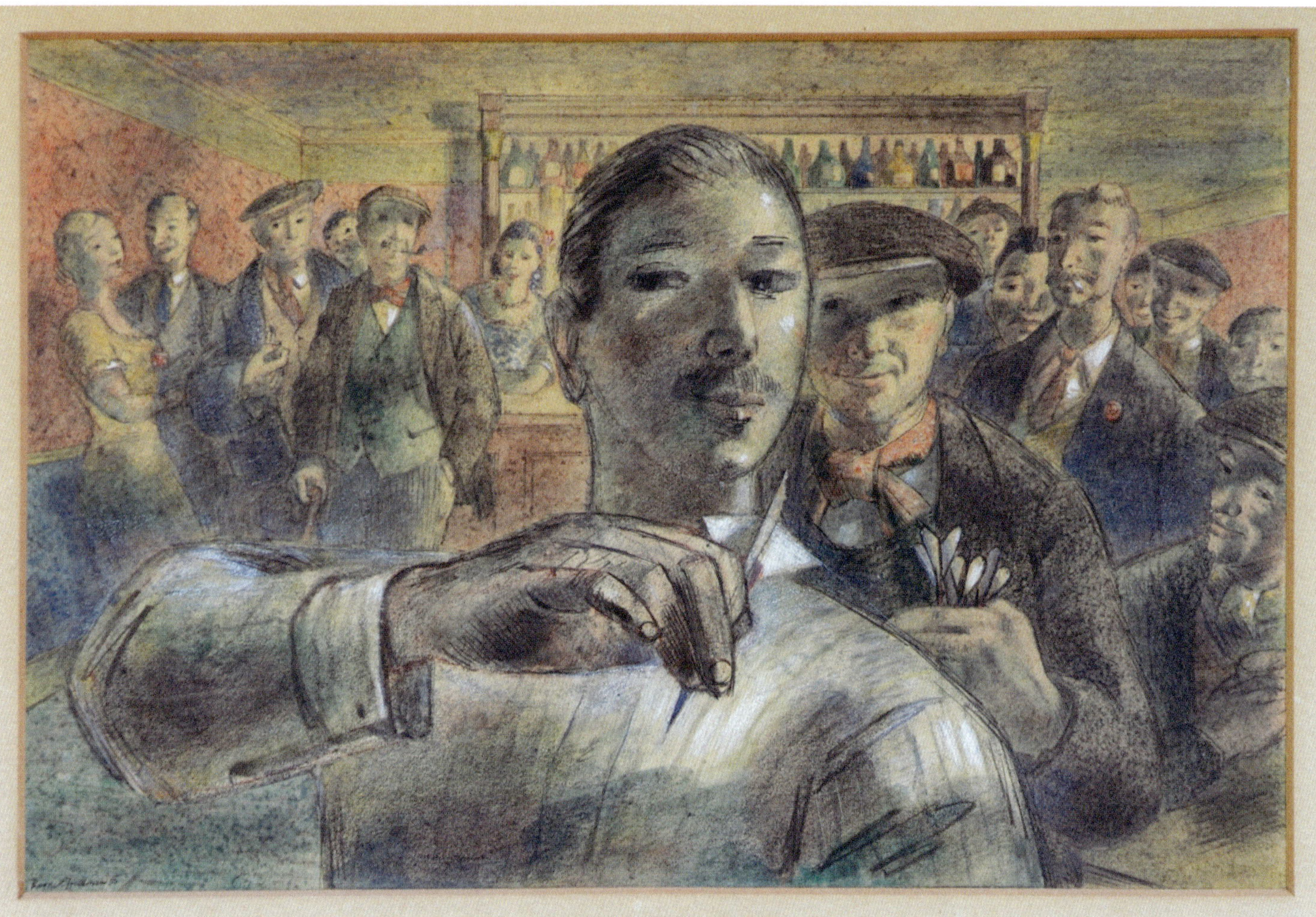

to create public works, bringing art to the masses. This was not a completely new thing as the Underground Division of London Transport had been commissioning artists to produce lithographs since the 1920s. For several decades prints had been seen pasted up in prominent places across the Underground with the projects largely overseen by the publicity manager at London Transport, Frank Pick (1878-1941).

Other large businesses such as the regional railways and Shell-Mex also employed artists to produce high quality publicity posters and prints. Shell-Mex commissioned artists under the guidance of their publicity manager, Jack Beddington, who was a great supporter of artists and he actively sought out new talent. He was committed to developing art for all, with his view that prints and posters were the most democratic art medium. Tommy Marks was fulfilling a similar role at Guinness and must have known about the successful projects and commissions created by Beddington at Shell-Mex and Pick at London Transport.

There are several lithography print-based series from the late 1930s to the late 1950s:

Contemporary Lithographs 1937-38

Artists' International Association's 'Everyman Prints' 1940

The School Prints 1946-49

The Festival of Britain Series 1951

Lyons Lithographs 1946-1955

The Coronation Series, from the Royal College of Art 1953

Wapping to Windsor Series, from the Royal College of Art 1957-58

Freedman's original pastel sketch for
The Darts Champion
Private Collection.

These print series share similarities through the artists involved, the imagery and the ways in which they were displayed in public spaces. Perhaps though it is:

'...only from hindsight that such efforts can be linked together not only by their direct or indirect intent, but by the artists involved (many contributing to more than one scheme), by the general content and style of the images (the British scene) and by their medium, lithography.' 11.

With these print series art was being brought out of galleries and into the public realm, available for all to see; posters in shop windows, glimpses of images on the sides of passing vehicles, prints displayed on the walls in tearooms, school or pubs. These schemes fulfilled the mid century idea of 'art for all'.

The Guinness Lithographs were a very important series sitting alongside these others, but they have often been overlooked. This is in the main because the prints rarely survived, having been pinned up or pasted on walls in pubs and later thrown away. Also there are so few records about the scheme and when I started my research no one seemed to have a full series of the lithographs. In the book *British Printmakers* by Garton & Co the series is listed but says that records are sparse with no complete list to confirm the details of prints in the series. Through our research we believe that we now have the full series.

Much of what we know about The Guinness Lithographs comes from the archives of the artists involved, in particular from Barnett Freedman's archives, which give us the background to his involvement in the project. From these we know that Barnett was meeting quite regularly with Tommy Marks and by March 1956 they were almost ready to go ahead with the scheme, with Marks writing:

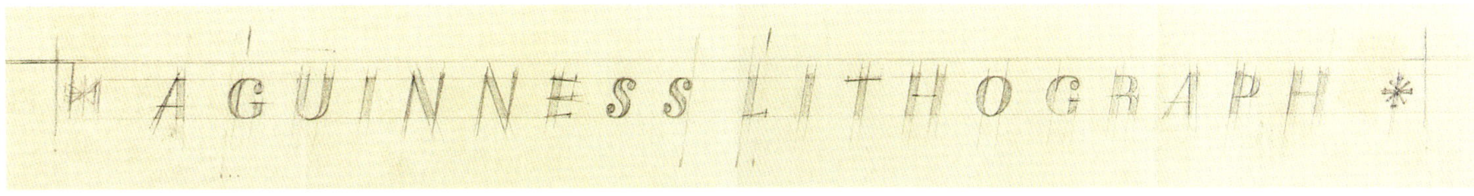

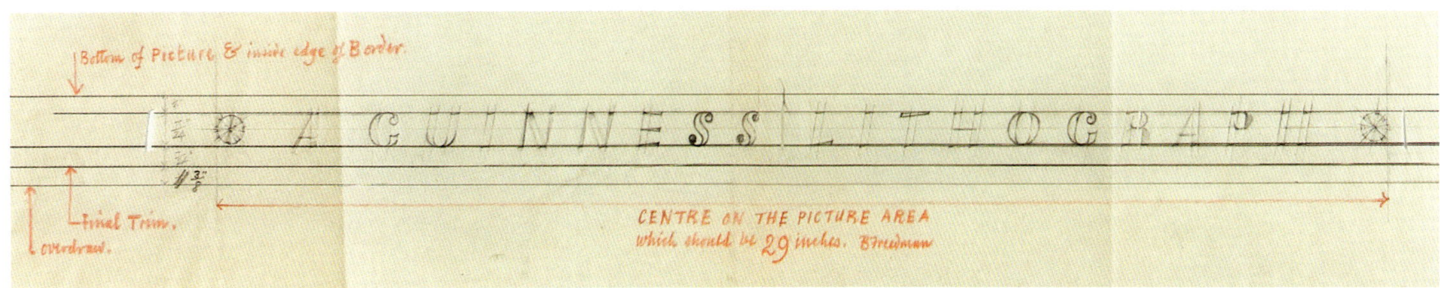

Lettering by Barnett Freedman
Courtesy of Manchester Metropolitan University
Special Collections.

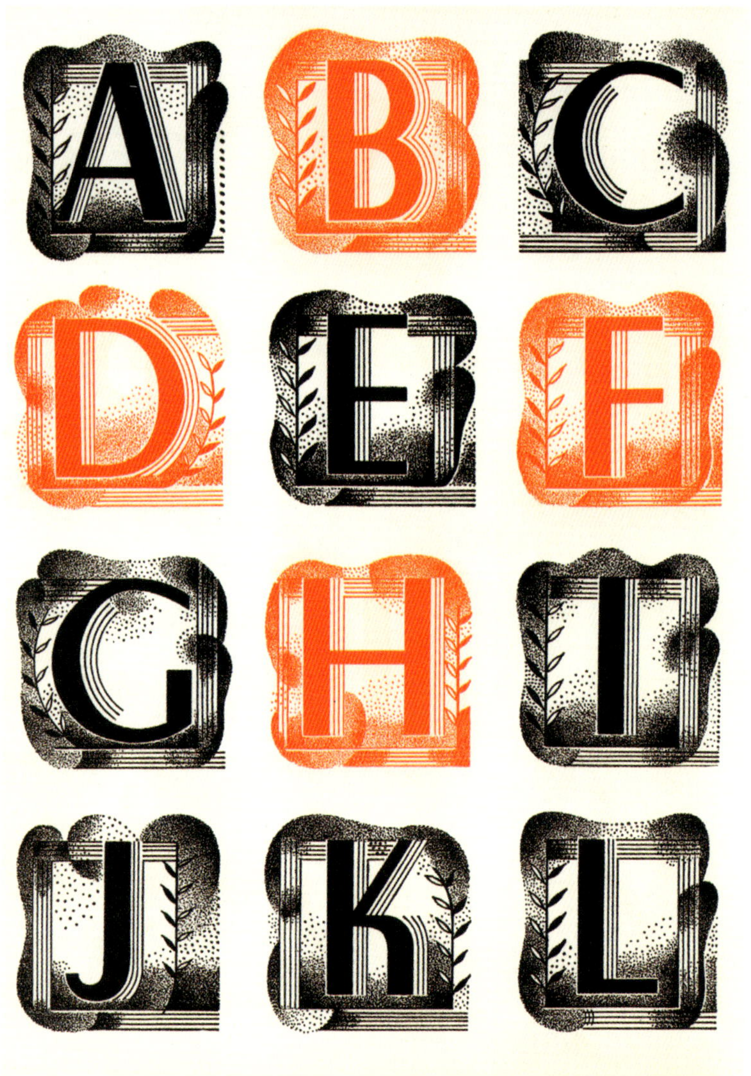

Baynard Claudia lettering by Barnett Freedman
Courtesy of Manchester Metropolitan University
Special Collections.

'Dear Barnett,

....I think we are now very nearly ready to go ahead with the scheme but before doing so I would like to have your final advice on size and format of the lithographs with particular reference to any border that you think should be incorporated.' 12.

Freedman advised on the size and design and the specification for the prints was decided on:

'...their final form will be 30" x 20", landscape shape. Allowing ½" margin all round the drawn area will measure 29" x 19". A small panel at the centre base will contain the necessary description of the work in transferred type.' 13.

The lithographs in the first series were therefore large, landscape shape with a small panel at the base of the image inscribed with the title of the image and name of the artist, followed by the words *Inspired by the Guinness Book of Records.* The lithographs were signed in the plate by the artist and inscribed The Curwen Press. Below the image is the lettering A Guinness Lithograph which was designed by Barnett Freedman. His archives contain drafts showing his workings for the lettering. Freedman was skilled in lettering and had experimented with different styles over the years especially with his beautiful designs for book jackets. He had designed his own lettering in 1935, which he named *Baynard Claudia* in honour of his wife.

The initial idea for the design of the lithographs was to have the panel below each image with not only the title but also a caption about which world record was being illustrated. This was later amended so in the final lithographs only the title is included.

The next step, a very important one, was to select the artists who were to be commissioned. It was agreed that there would be six artists initially and that at least two of the artists chosen should *not* have been involved in the earlier Lyons Series. The initial list put forward included Edwin La Dell, Ruskin Spear, Edward Ardizzone, David Gentleman, Sam Rabin and Barnett Freedman, who had said from the outset that he would like to make one of the lithographs. We do not know for certain which artists were short-listed or if any turned down the commission but we do know that many of the artists were connected to the Royal College of Art (RCA). We know that Sam Rabin and Ruskin Spear did not work on the series and that David Gentleman worked later on a lithograph for the second series. For the first series, in addition to Edwin La Dell, Edward Ardizzone and Barnett Freedman, all lecturers at the RCA, the three other artists who were chosen were Bernard Cheese, Brian Robb and Ronald Glendening. Both Cheese and Glendening were recent students at the RCA. Robb was a lecturer at the Chelsea School of Art, although he worked in later years at the RCA. These last three were artists who had not been involved in the Lyons Series. Other than Brian Robb they were all students or staff at the RCA and they would have known each other and each other's work.

Also a number of the artists involved were already known to have worked with Guinness Breweries such as Edward Ardizzone who had designed posters and booklets for Guinness a few years earlier.

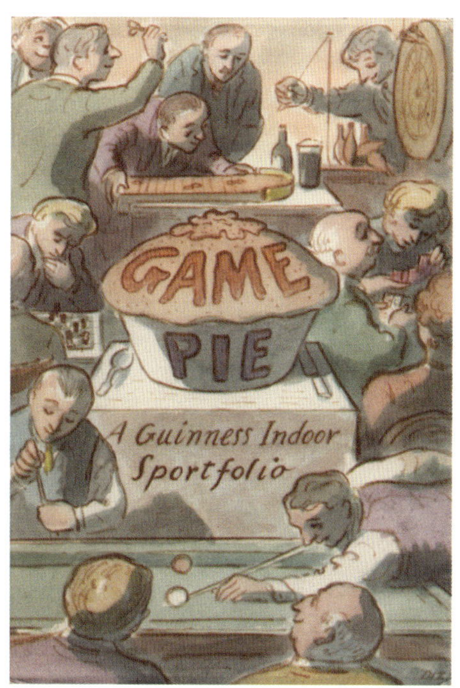

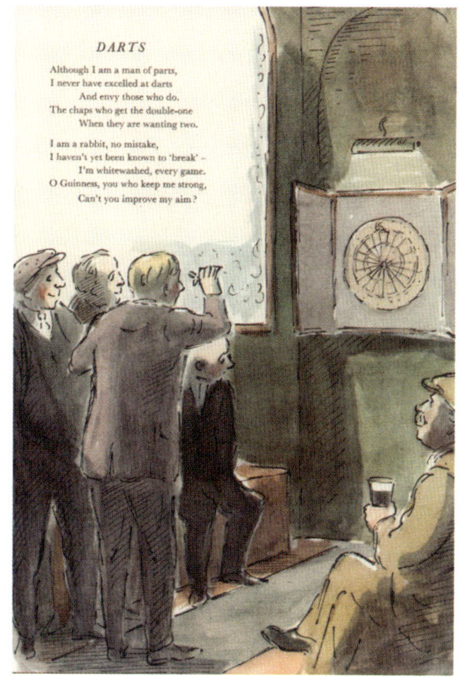

A Guinness Indoor Sportfolio 1955 illustrated by
Edward Ardizzone.

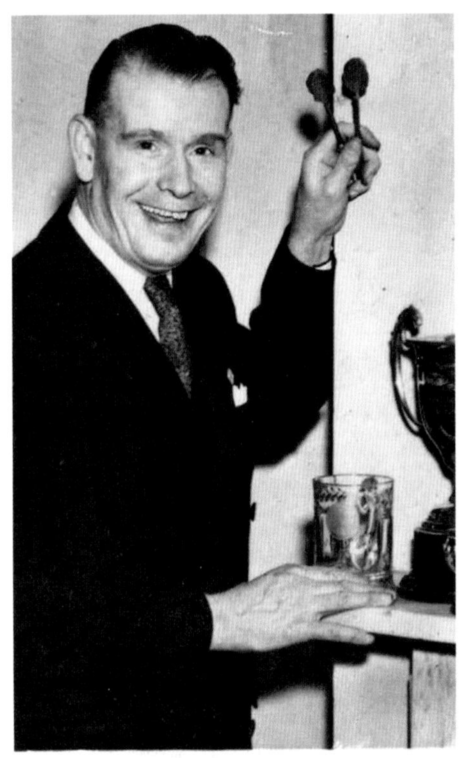

Jim Pike, Darts Champion.

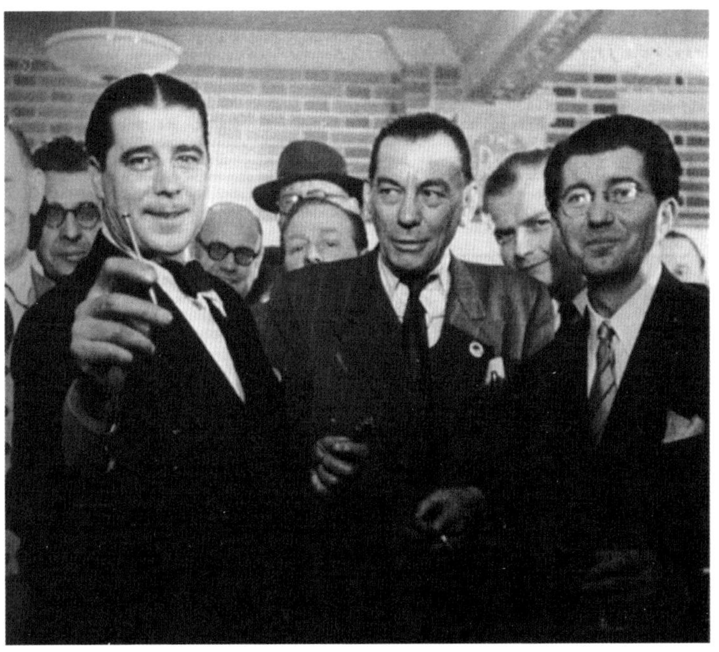

Joe Hitchcock, Darts Champion, seen here throwing nails as part of his darts exhibition.

Images courtesy of Dr Patrick Chaplin, Darts Historian.

Once the selected artists had accepted the commission, they were given details of the project, type of image required and the process involved. Each artist was given a copy of the first *Book of World Records* from which they were to choose a world record to illustrate. They were asked to choose the subject and design carefully as the lithographs were to be put up in public houses, working men's clubs and works canteens with the purpose of brightening up the often very drab surroundings whilst at the same time advertise the *Guinness Book of Records* to a wider audience. This is clearly set out by Marks in his letter to the artists:

'I would stress the fact that the lithographs are to be displayed on the walls of clubs and public houses, and the extent of their display will depend entirely on how well the recipients like them. I think therefore that the subject will have to be treated in a representational style, with a touch of lightness and humour where possible and that the colours chosen should be such that they will contrast with the somewhat drab surroundings in which a number of them will appear.' 14.

The images needed to appeal to the audience in the pubs and have a subject matter that might be debated by those enjoying a drink. The images chosen reflect the interest in working class culture at the time, epitomised by John Osborne's *Look Back in Anger* of 1956. As such the themes of darts, horse racing, pigeon racing, football and fishing were among the subjects chosen by the artists.

Brian Robb illustrated a popular place for a day out in the 1950s, Southend Pier the longest pleasure pier in the world. Two of the artists, Bernard Cheese and Barnett Freedman, chose to make images of scenes set in a pub, which make their lithographs particularly suited to their purpose. In his lithograph *A Fisherman's Story,* Bernard Cheese shows his wry sense of humour as he captures the moment a fisherman is boasting about his catch, arms outstretched, whilst on the bar next to him there are some tiny fish.

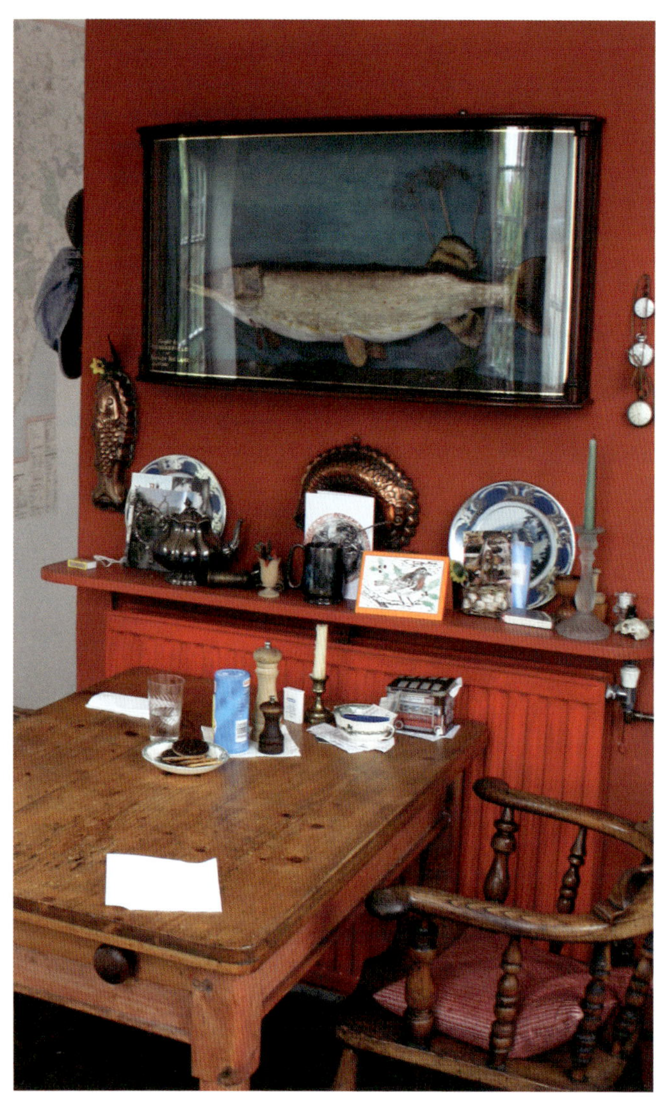

Bernard Cheese's kitchen, Nayland, Essex, 2010
Photo Emma Mason.

The fish in the glass case on the wall of the pub in his lithograph is similar to one that Cheese had in his own home for many years. In *The Darts Champion* Barnett Freedman illustrates the popular pub game. The man throwing the darts is very similar to either champion of the day, and record holder Jim Pike, or more likely his adversary Joe Hitchcock, as Jim Pike was not known to have sported a moustache. The images also had to be bright and attractive to work well on the walls of often smoky and dimly lit pubs, bars and canteens. There are some wonderful colours in all the lithographs such as the reds and greens in *Newmarket* by Edwin La Dell and the bright emerald green of the pub in *A Fisherman's Story* by Bernard Cheese. The prints would have looked impressive on the walls and would have created a talking point that in turn brought people to look at the *Guinness Book of Records*.

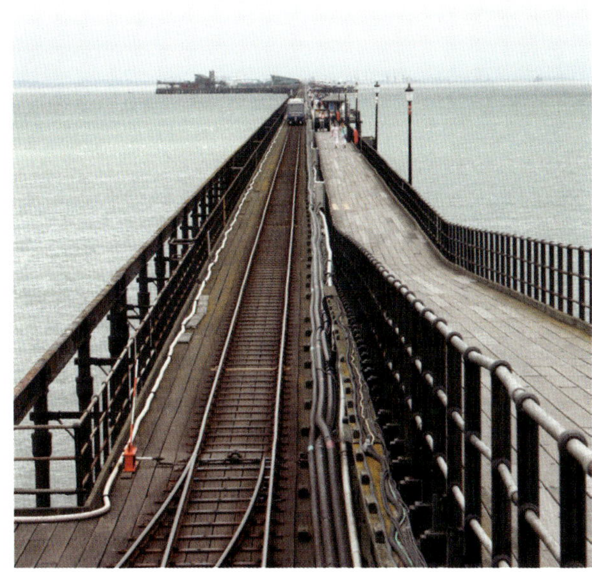

Southend Pier today.
Photo Emma Mason.

The final six artists commissioned for the first series were:

Edward Ardizzone

Bernard Cheese

Barnett Freedman

Ronald Glendening

Edwin La Dell

Brian Robb

The artists proposed an idea for their image and once Guinness had agreed to the subject matter the artist submitted a sketch of the subject, a rough sketch being adequate at this stage. With the sketch accepted the artist would then carry out their lithography. In the first series each artist was paid a sum of £50 for the initial sketch and a further £150 for the lithography. There was quite a tight timescale with the artists having just a couple of months to have the finished proof ready, with a deadline of 1st June 1956.

All the images for both the first series and the second series were made as lithographs and the choice of lithography fitted the needs of the scheme very well. In the post-war years the process of lithography was seen as an excellent method of colour reproduction, a well needed antidote to the war economy of monotone printing.

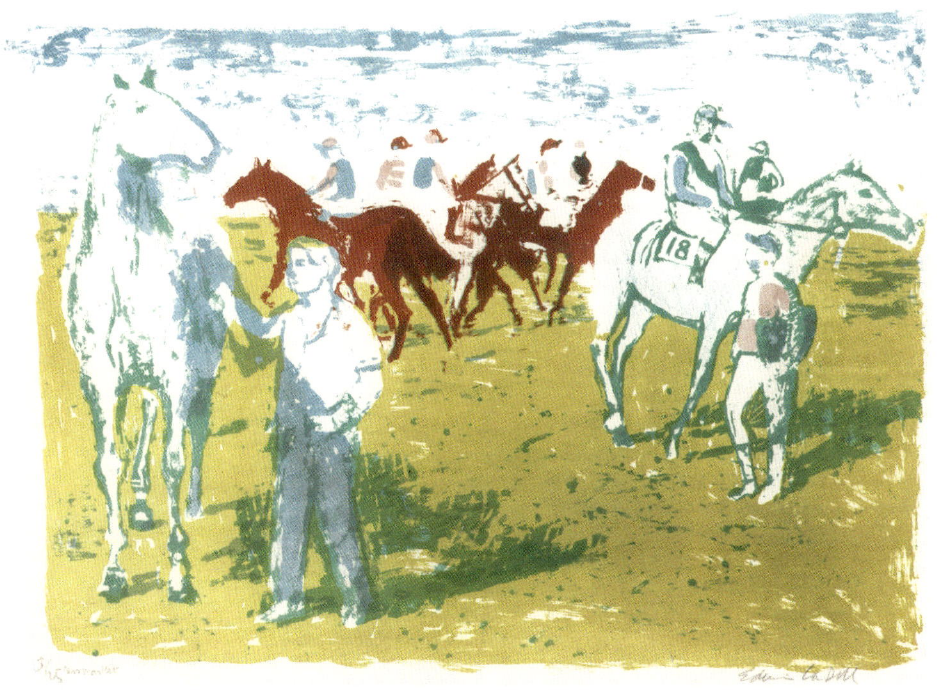

Edwin La Dell *Newmarket,* lithograph

Lithography became the main commercial printing method of the time. The artist could work directly on to the lithographic stone or plate and this suited the needs of larger-scale work for posters or prints. This method, called auto-lithography, suited those artists who were skilled in lithography as they understood the process and were comfortable drawing directly on the plate.

However, lithography is a complicated process and some of the artists had little experience of it. For these artists they used a different approach where the artist worked with highly trained interpretive lithography technicians from commercial printing companies. These technicians would have the artist's image to work from, usually a painting. They would carefully copy the original artwork transposing it into a lithograph. This worked perfectly in many instances but in others the detail of the original image was lost. To a large extent the success or otherwise of the final lithograph was dependent on the artist producing an image which could be successfully recreated from a canvas to a lithograph.

Barnett Freedman was the ideal person to oversee the scheme as he was considered a master of the technique of lithography, often referred to as the lithographer's lithographer. With both the earlier project for the Lyons Lithographs and the Guinness Series observers would perhaps suggest that the most successful images are those that were auto-lithographed by the artist. There is certainly more confidence in the images made by those artists who were skilled in auto-lithography ie Freedman, La Dell, Cheese, Ardizzone.

Barnett Freedman recognised the growing opportunities that auto-lithography provided for artists describing auto-lithography as:

'...the real sphere for the future activities of artists who are prepared to overcome the difficulties of working in close co-operation with publishers and printing houses. These difficulties are considerable and derive mainly from the printing trade's apprehension lest original artists producing their own lithography ultimately become competitors of professional copyists and photomechanical photo operatives. This narrow and restricted view can only be sustained through a false understanding of the fundamental fact that while reproductions produced either by photomechanical means or by skilled hand copyists are necessary and valuable commodities fulfilling a most useful function for a multitude of purposes, autolithographs – the direct outcome of the work of original artists on lithographic stones – are works of art in their own right.' 15.

Freedman advised Guinness on all the technical aspects involved in the project for the first series and he suggested that they work with Curwen Press in Plaistow, London a specialist lithography studio:

'The Curwen Press has an unusual regard for the artists who worked with the firm. While many printing houses were satisfied with approximations to the artist's palette, the Curwen Press acknowledged the integrity of the artist and made considerable effort to achieve exact reproduction.' 16.

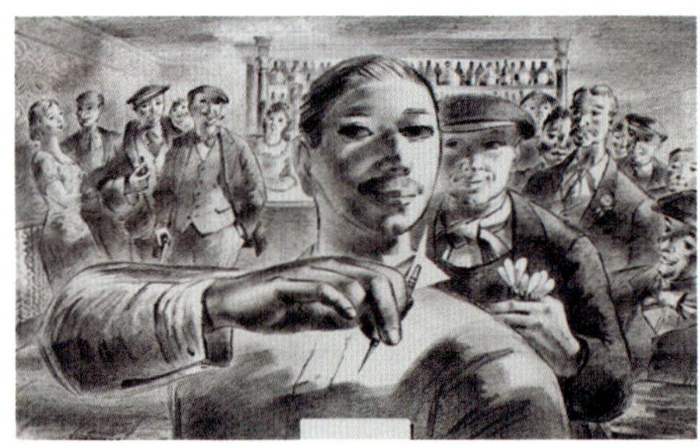
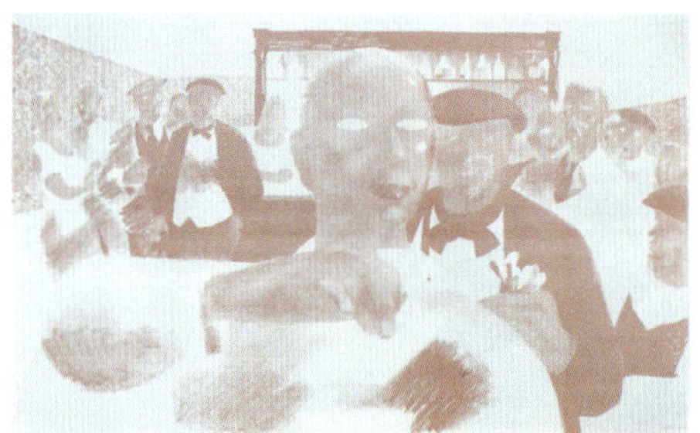

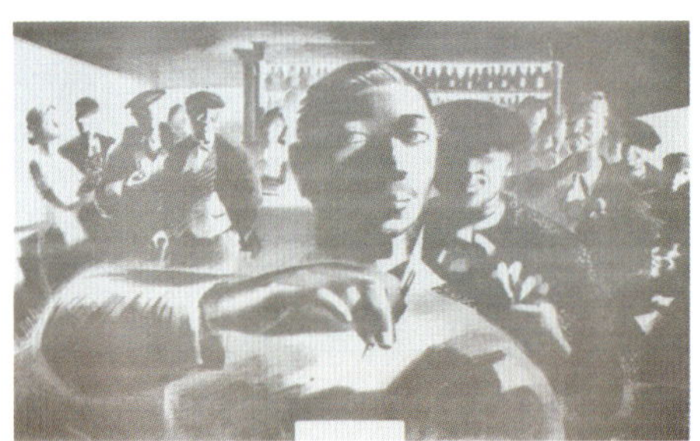
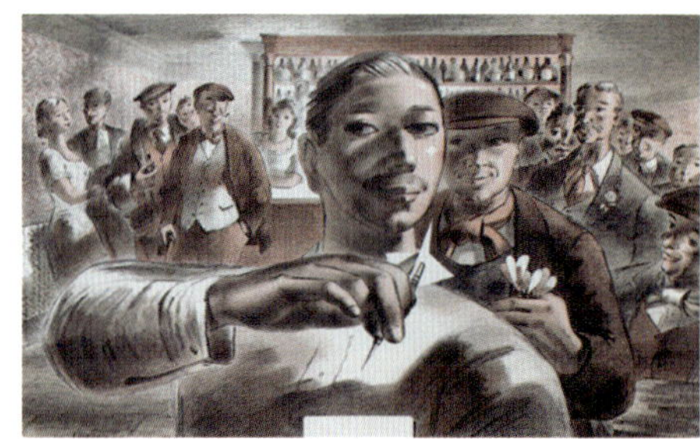

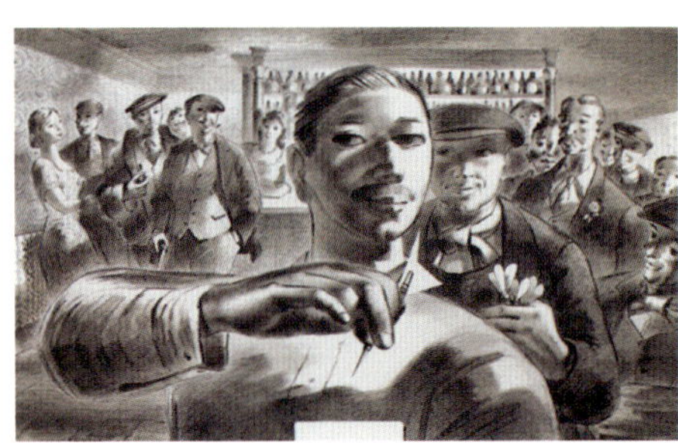
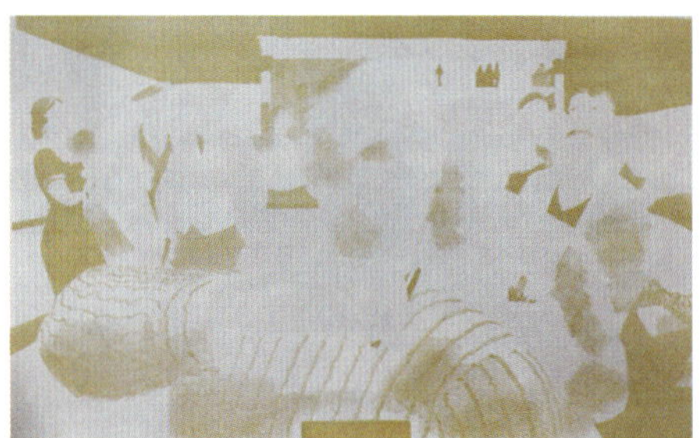

The twelve colour separations for the
The Darts Champion by Barnett Freedman
Courtesy of Michael S Kemp, Bookseller.

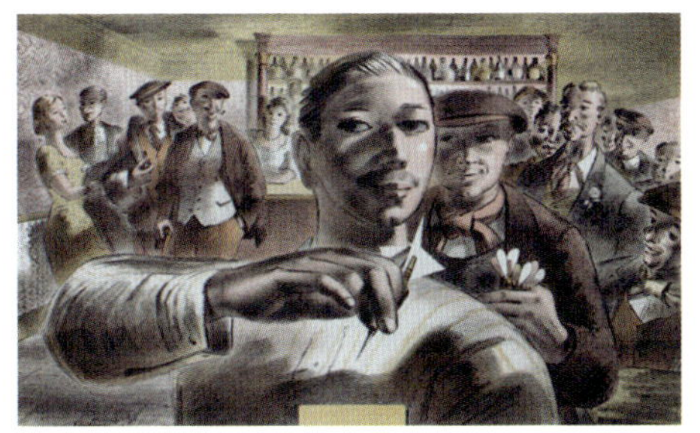
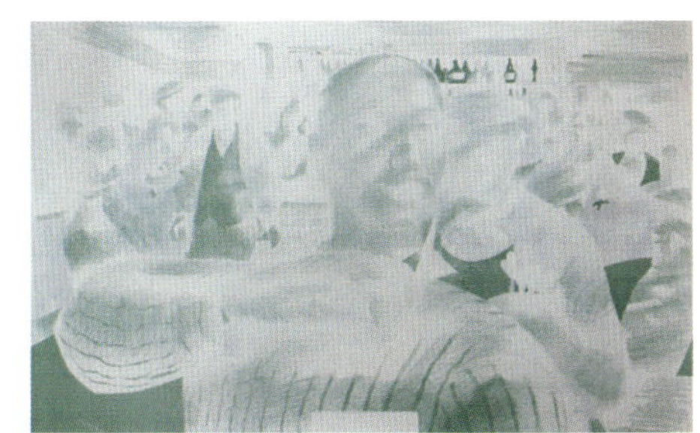
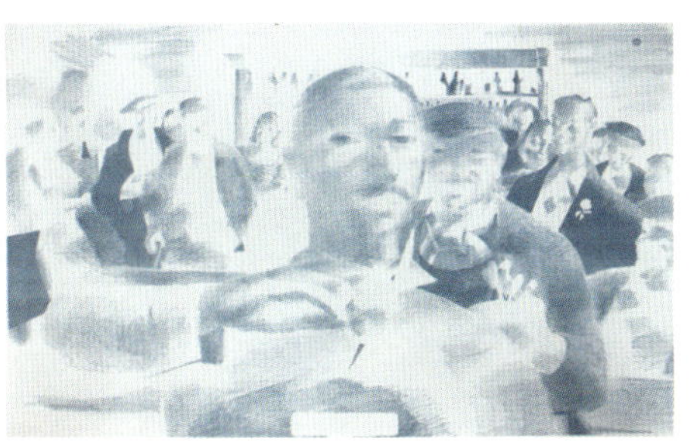
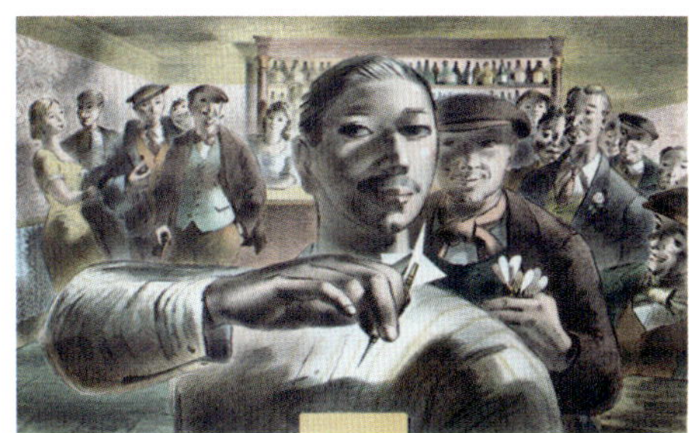
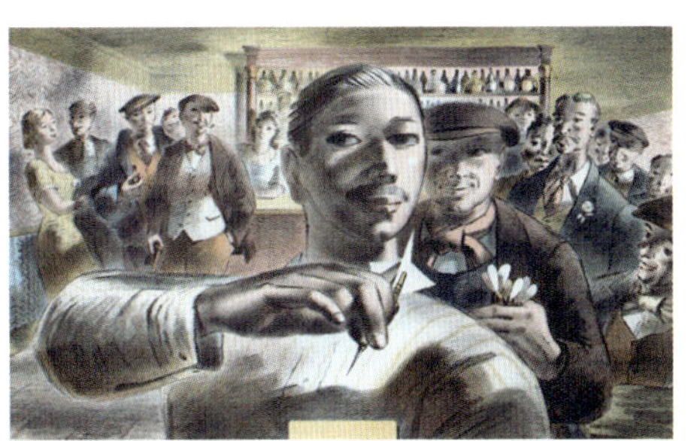
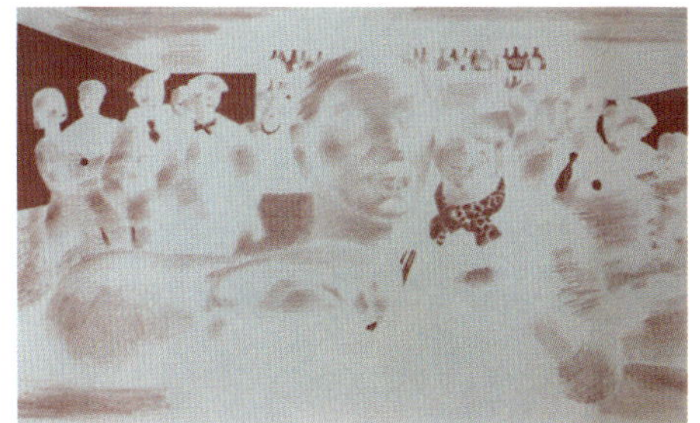

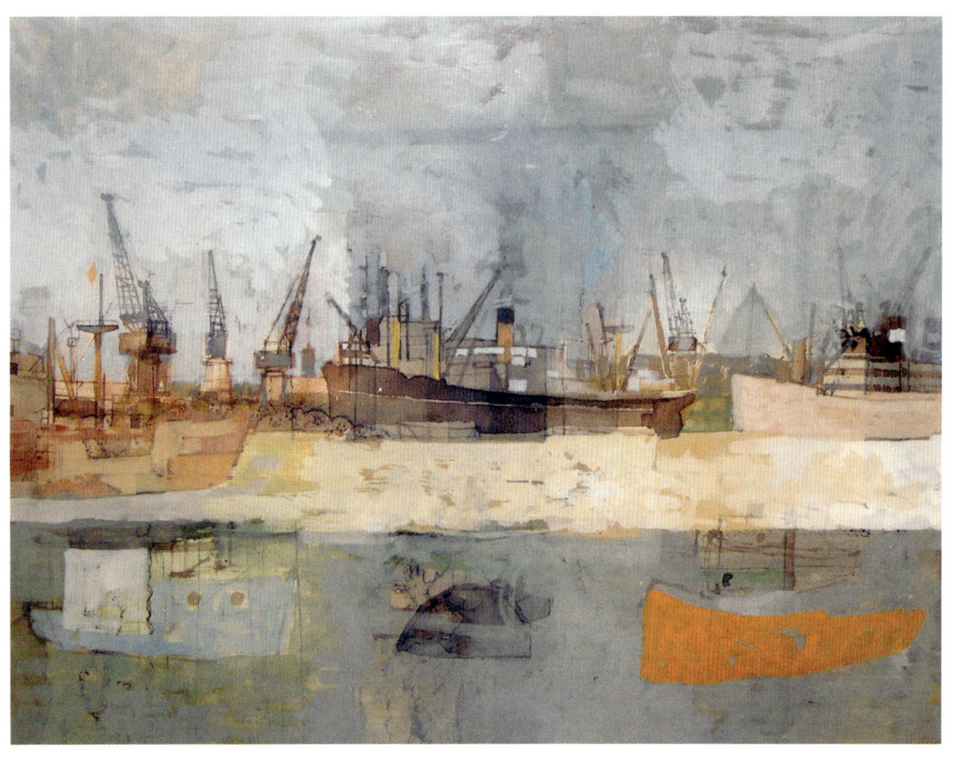

Original painting, *Royal Albert Dock, London*, 1962
by Leonard Rosomon
Image courtesy of A Phelps.

The second series of lithographs were commissioned a few years later in 1962 by which time the *Guinness Book of Records* was fully established and very successful. There has been some confusion about the date for the second series and it has been listed as 1957. However, our research shows that the second series was commissioned in 1962 and the original works of art that have come to light have been signed and dated 1962. Barnett Freedman was not involved in the second series as he died in 1958 at the age of only fifty-seven. He had continued to work as an advisor to Guinness until he died, meeting with them over dinner once every couple of months. We do not have records about who oversaw this later series but we can assume that Tommy Marks was still the main person at Guinness with responsibility for commissioning the second series.

As with the first series, the second involved six artists and again they all had connections with the Royal College of Art (RCA). Two of the chosen artists were recent students from the RCA; David Gentleman and Rosamund Steed, and the other four were teaching staff. The artists for the second series were:

David Gentleman

Alistair Grant

Richard Guyatt

Leonard Rosoman

Rosamund Steed

Carel Weight

As with the earlier series the artists used the book of world records from which they chose a subject to illustrate. David Gentleman chose to illustrate the world record for the oldest rowing race. He recalls working on the commission in 1962 and remembers going to look at the actual ceremonial coat and badge worn by the watermen at Fishmonger's Hall. Gentleman had only produced three lithographs previously, two for posters whilst a student at the Royal College of Art and one of a Cornish pilchard boat for the Lyons Lithographs in 1953-4.

Gentleman recalls how he auto-lithographed his image, on zinc plates, which he drew in his studio. The plates were then taken to Curwen Press in Plaistow where they were proofed and printed.

Rosamund Steed remembers how she went to Ireland and stopped off at Cork where she saw the sailing club. She made some drawings and was pleased to have found a subject to illustrate for the Guinness lithograph series, Cork being the oldest yacht club in the world.

The second series of lithographs followed a similar path to the first series with images of subjects popular with the audience in the pubs of the day, particularly the images of football, pigeon racing, the docks and a pleasure pier.

The lithographs were smaller in size to the first series and measure 38cm x 50cm. They did not have the label along the bottom but just had the panel, which gave the title, the artist and the line *Inspired by the Guinness Book of Records*. By the time the second series was published in 1962 the *Guinness Book of Records* was so successful it required less publicity and this perhaps explains why the lithographs were smaller and lacked the border and lettering.

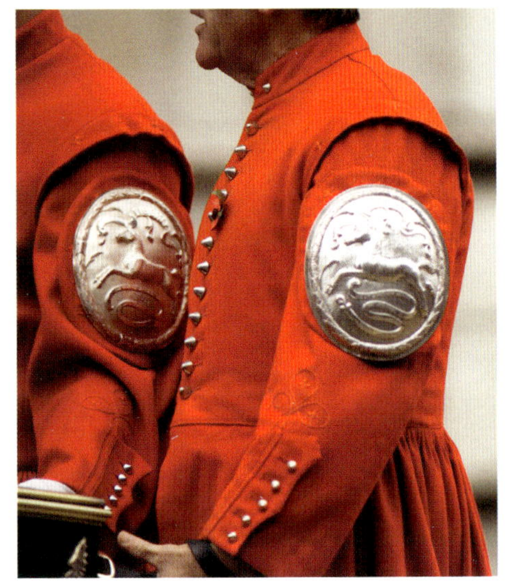

Doggett's Coat and Badge Men
© Malcolm Park London events / Alamy.

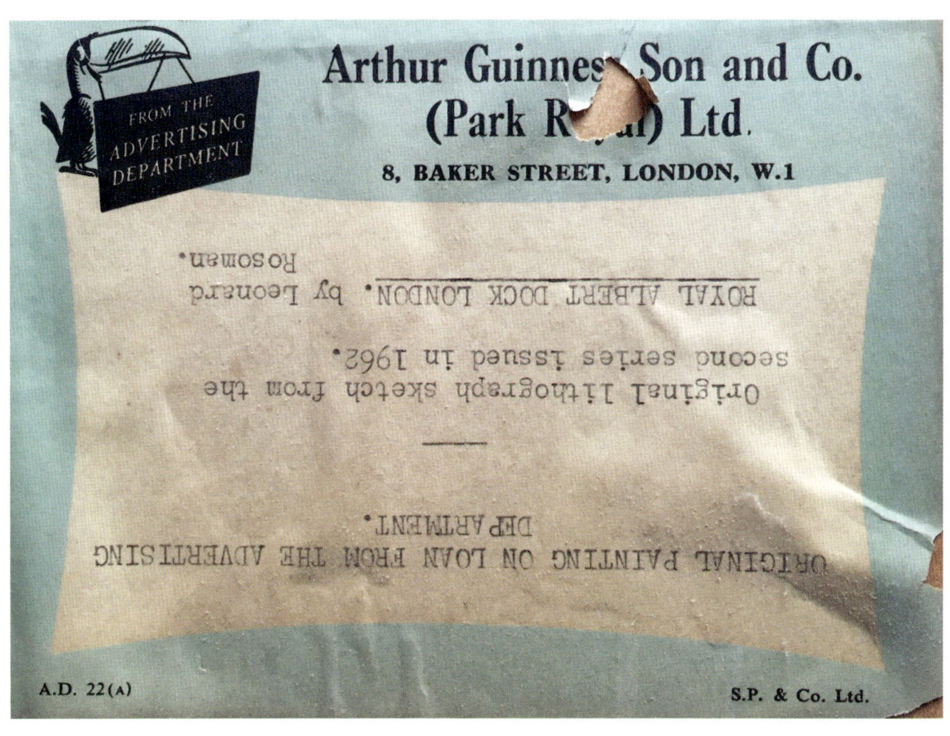

Label on the back of Leonard Rosoman's painting, *Royal Albert Dock, London*

Image courtesy of A Phelps.

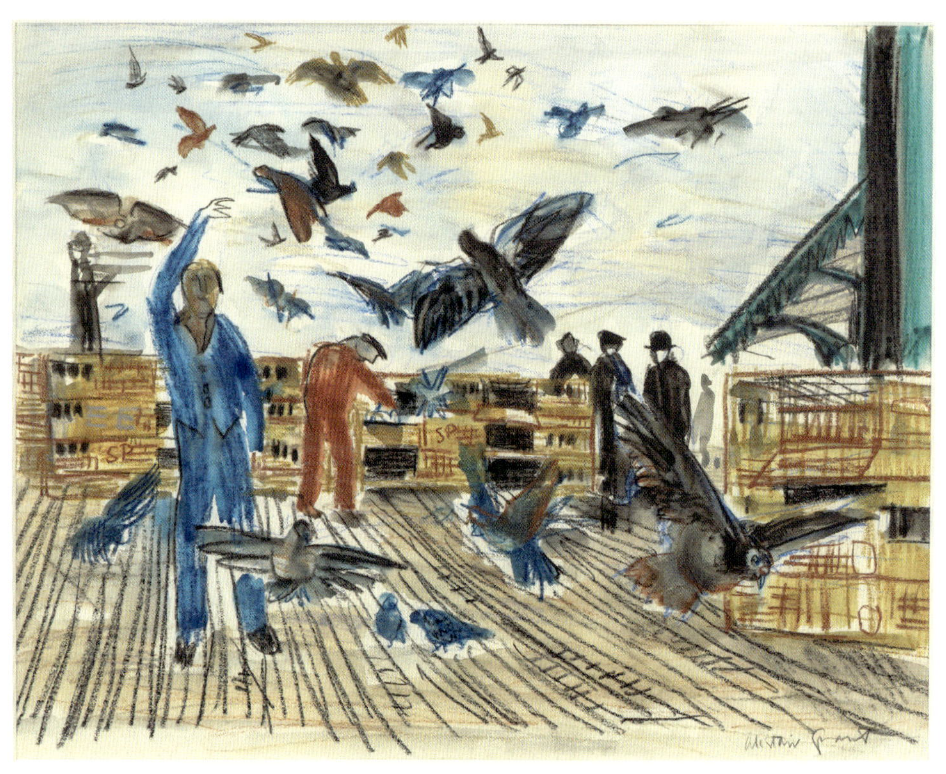

Original watercolour by Alistair Grant for his
lithograph *Pigeon Racing*
Courtesy of Emma Mason.

Although there are only twelve prints in the Guinness Lithograph series they are an important addition to the group of lithography-based print series produced in Britain in the post-war years. The Guinness series has been largely forgotten because, as with similar projects, the lithographs were seen as ephemeral objects and were pinned on walls and then after time thrown away. The Guinness Lithographs were made for pubs and working men's clubs and as such probably survived even less well than the lithographs displayed in the cleaner environments of schools and tearooms. We do not know for certain how many of the Guinness Lithographs were printed but those that have survived are often in poor condition. The other reason for the story having been overlooked has been the lack of records available and most of what we now know has come from the artists and their own archives.

The Guinness Lithographs demonstrate the interest of the time in 'art for all' and the role that printmaking in Britain could offer to the democratisation of art in the post-war years. They also provide a strong sense of social history with images that capture the everyday life of people, their conversations, and interests taking place in pubs across the country. It is the combination of the images and the story behind them that make the Guinness Lithographs so unique.

* A GUINNESS LITHOGRAPH *

The Guinness Lithographs
First Series
1956

The Fattest Woman in the World

Lithograph, image size 48cm x 73.5cm

Edward Ardizzone (1900-79)

Originally called *The Heaviest Woman in the World.* Ardizzone illustrated the record for the world's heaviest recorded woman as described in the section for Heaviest Heavyweights in The Human Being chapter.

The Guinness Book of Records 1955 p.39

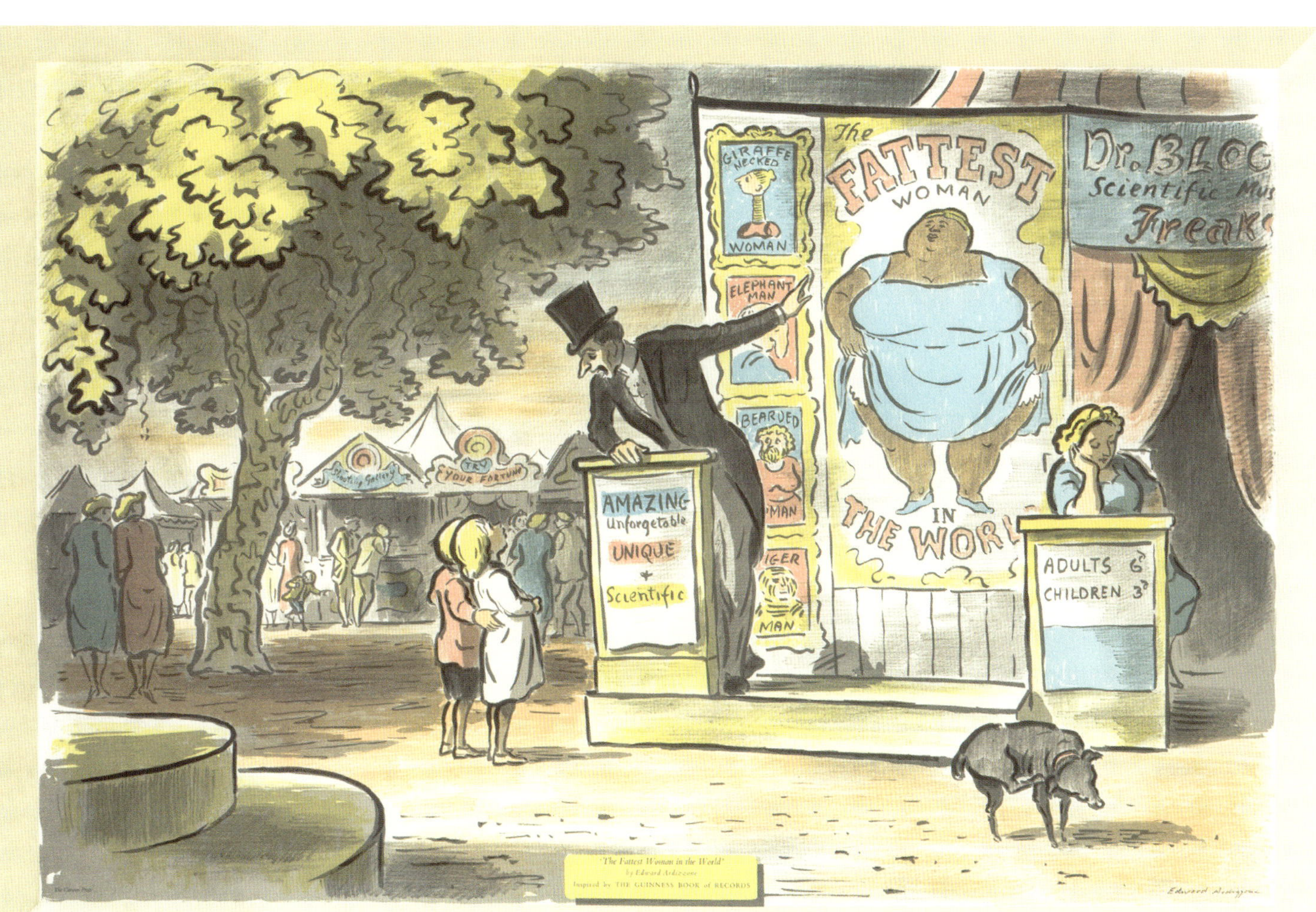

'The Fattest Woman in the World'
by Edward Ardizzone
Inspired by THE GUINNESS BOOK of RECORDS

Edward Ardizzone

A Fisherman's Story

Lithograph, image size 48cm x 73.5cm

Bernard Cheese (1925-2013)

Originally called *Angling,* Cheese illustrated an image from the Angling, Largest Catches section in the Sport chapter. Cheese uses his sharp sense of humour to place his characters in a pub setting with the fisherman, arms outstretched, boasting about his catch. Meanwhile some tiny fish are shown on a newspaper on the bar. The image of the fish in the glass case was taken from one that Cheese had in his own home.

The Guinness Book of Records 1955 p.151

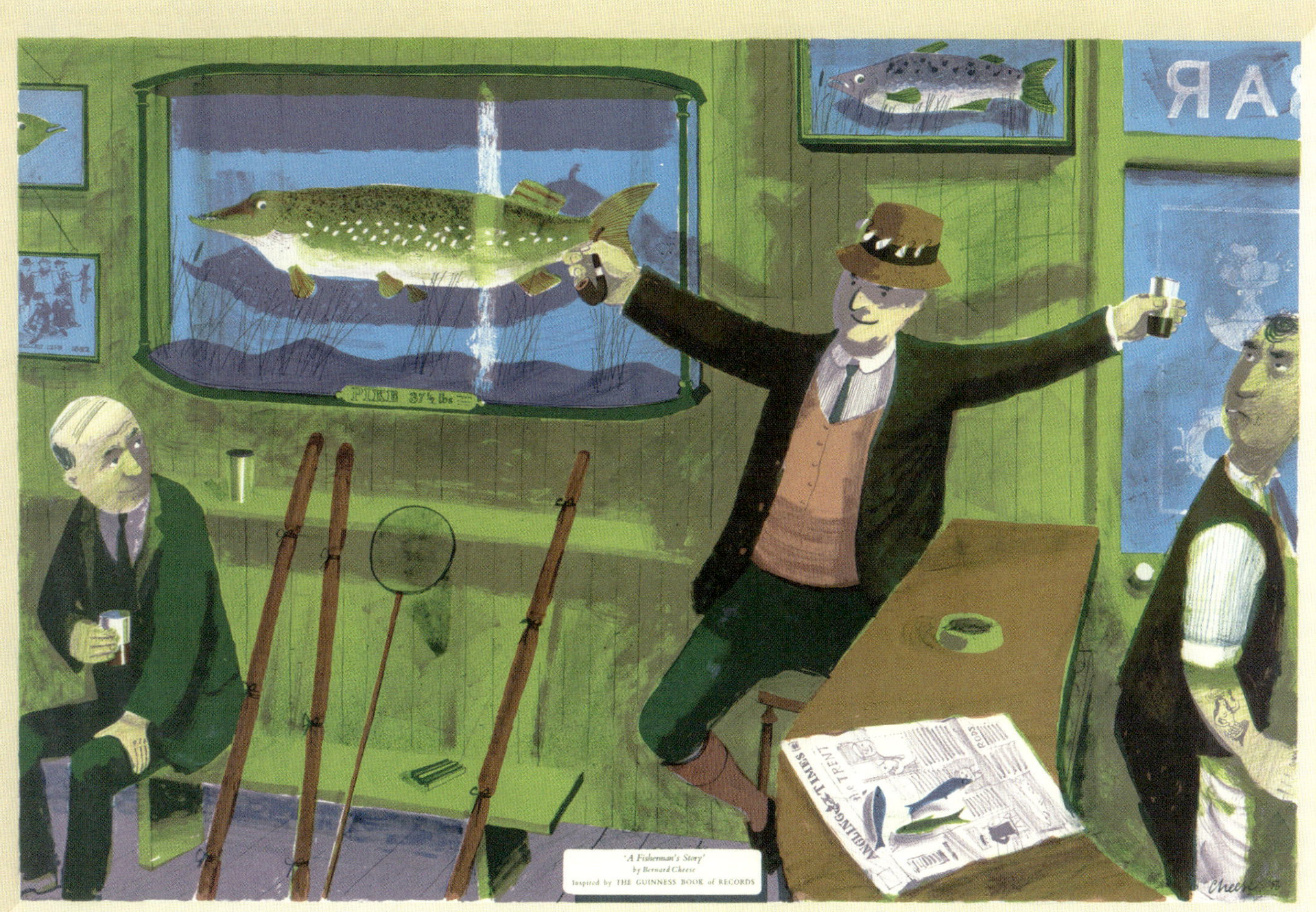
PIKE 37½ lbs
BAR
ANGLING TIMES
The TRENT
'A Fisherman's Story'
by Bernard Cheese
Inspired by THE GUINNESS BOOK of RECORDS
Cheese

* A GUINNESS LITHOGRAPH *

The Darts Champion

Lithograph, image size 48cm x 73.5cm

Barnett Freedman (1901-58)

Freedman chose an image well suited to pub life, the darts champion. He based his image on the Darts section in the Sports chapter. The image is based on records by darts champions of the day such as Jim Pike, who held the records for fastest round the board and fastest match:

'The fastest time taken for a match of three games of 301 is 2½ minutes by Jim Pike at Broadcasting House, Broad Street, Birmingham in 1952.'

The Guinness Book of Records 1955 p.167

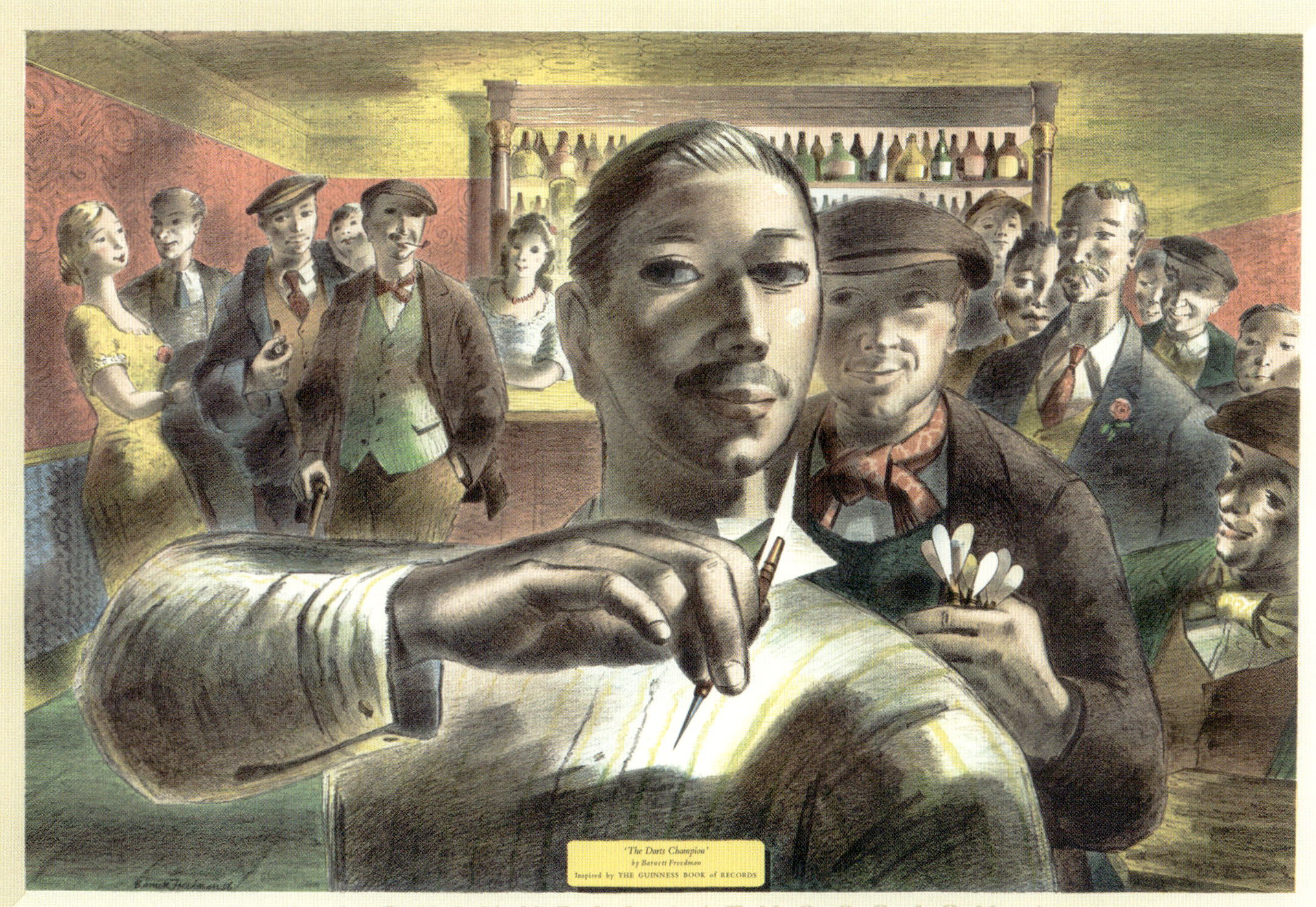

* A GUINNESS LITHOGRAPH *

Cycle Racing

Lithograph, image size 48cm x 73.5cm

Ronald Glendening (1926-2013)

Originally called *Racing Cyclists* Glendening based his lithograph on the world records listed for Cycling in the Sport chapter.

The Guinness Book of Records 1955 p.165

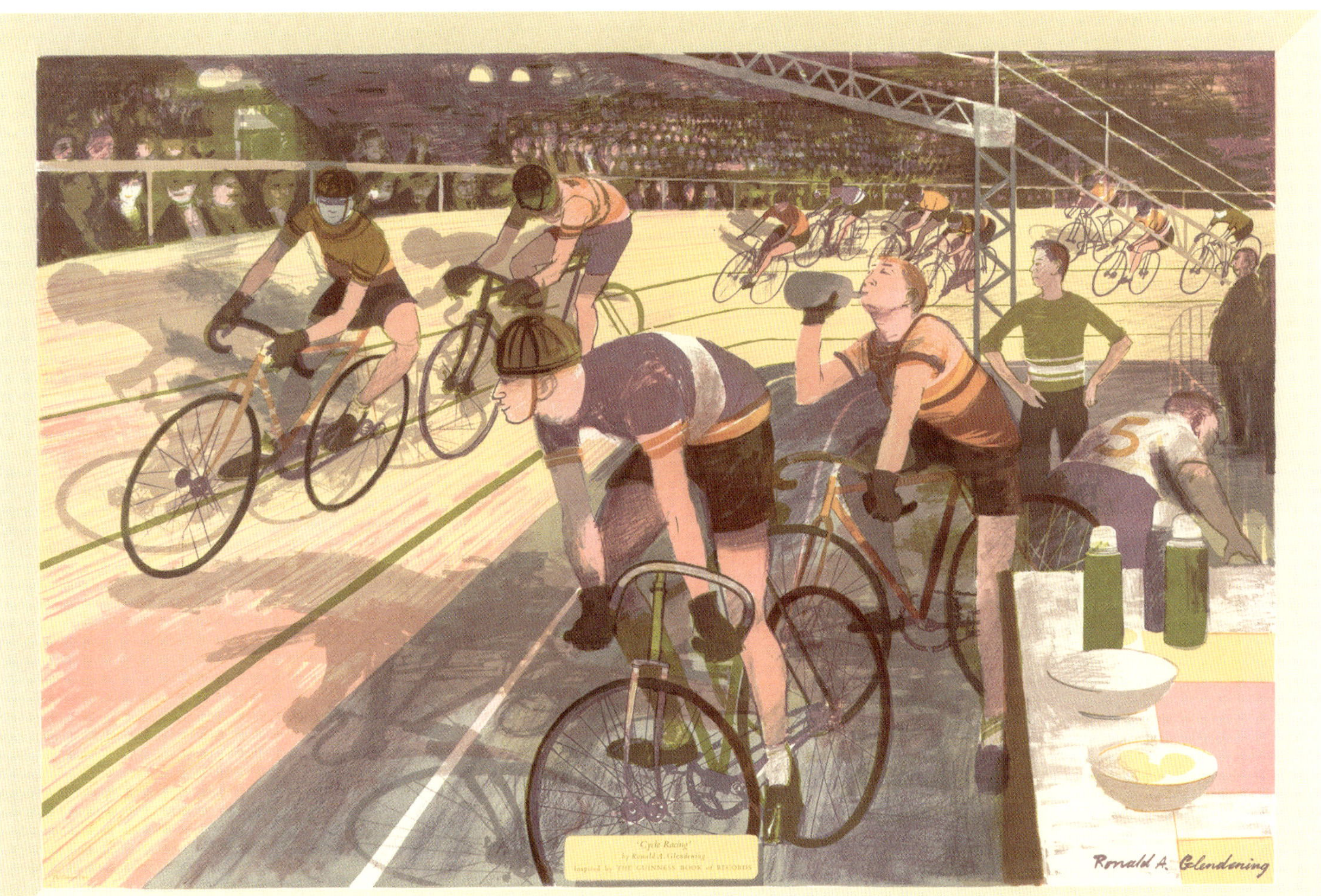

'Cycle Racing'
by Ronald A. Glendening
Inspired by THE GUINNESS BOOK of RECORDS
Ronald A. Glendening
* A GUINNESS LITHOGRAPH *

Newmarket

Lithograph, image size 48cm x 73.5cm

Edwin La Dell (1914-70)

Originally the title was *Newmarket Races* but was shortened to just *Newmarket*. La Dell chose a subject relevant to the pub audience. His lithograph is from the Sport chapter in the section on Horse Racing. It shows Newmarket, which held the record as the world's largest racecourse:

'The world's largest racecourse is the 320 year old Newmarket, Cambridgeshire, England on which the Beacon course is 4 miles 397 yards long and the Rowley Mile is 167 feet wide.'

The Guinness Book of Records 1955 p.174

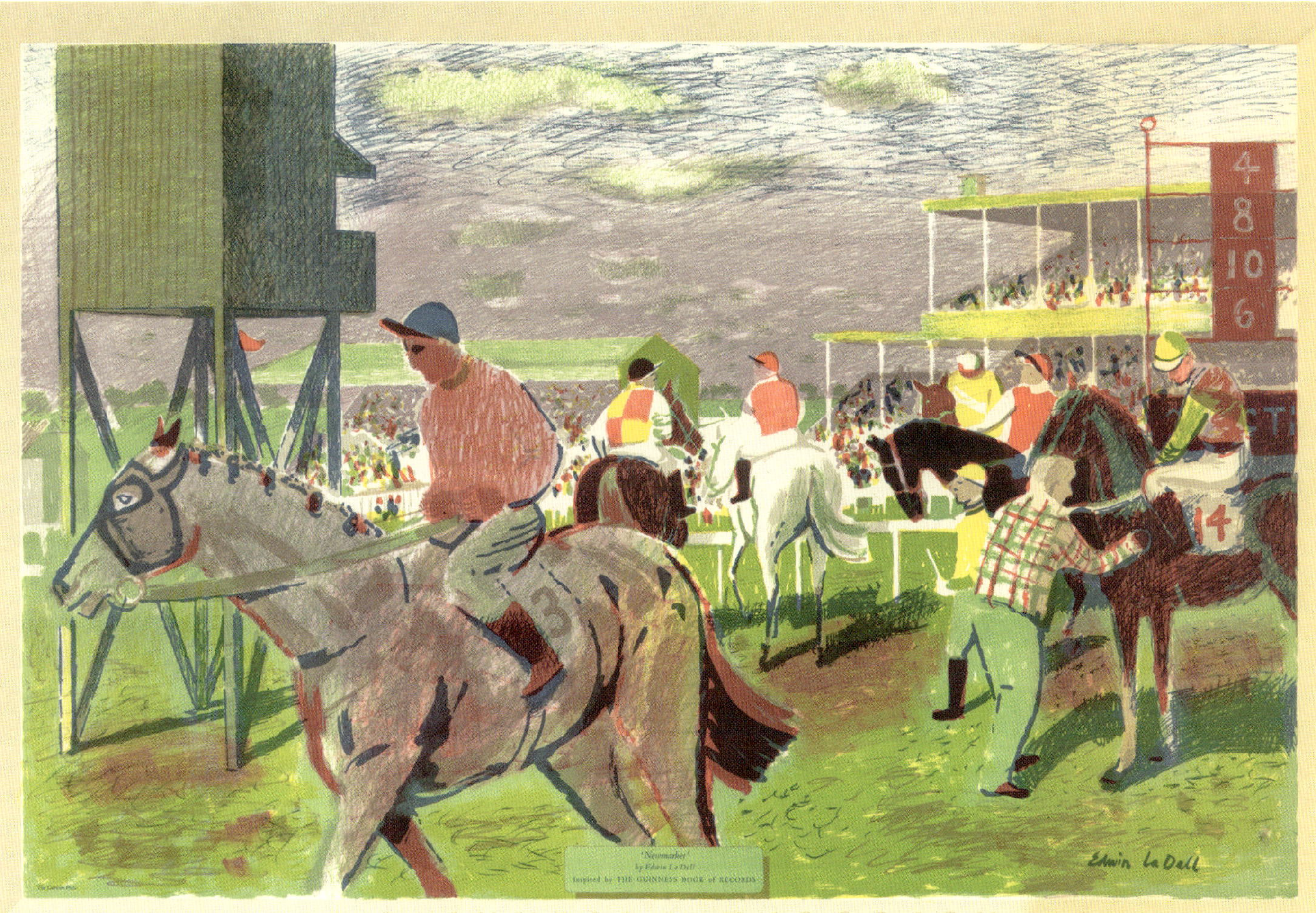

* A GUINNESS LITHOGRAPH *

Southend Pier

Lithograph, image size 48cm x 73.5cm

Brian Robb (1913-79)

Robb chose a subject from the chapter The World's Structures and he illustrated one close to home, a British world record holder, the world's longest pleasure pier, Southend Pier:

'The longest pleasure pier in the world is Southend Pier, $1\frac{1}{3}$ miles in length. It is decorated with more than 75,000 lamps.'

The Guinness Book of Records 1955 p.101

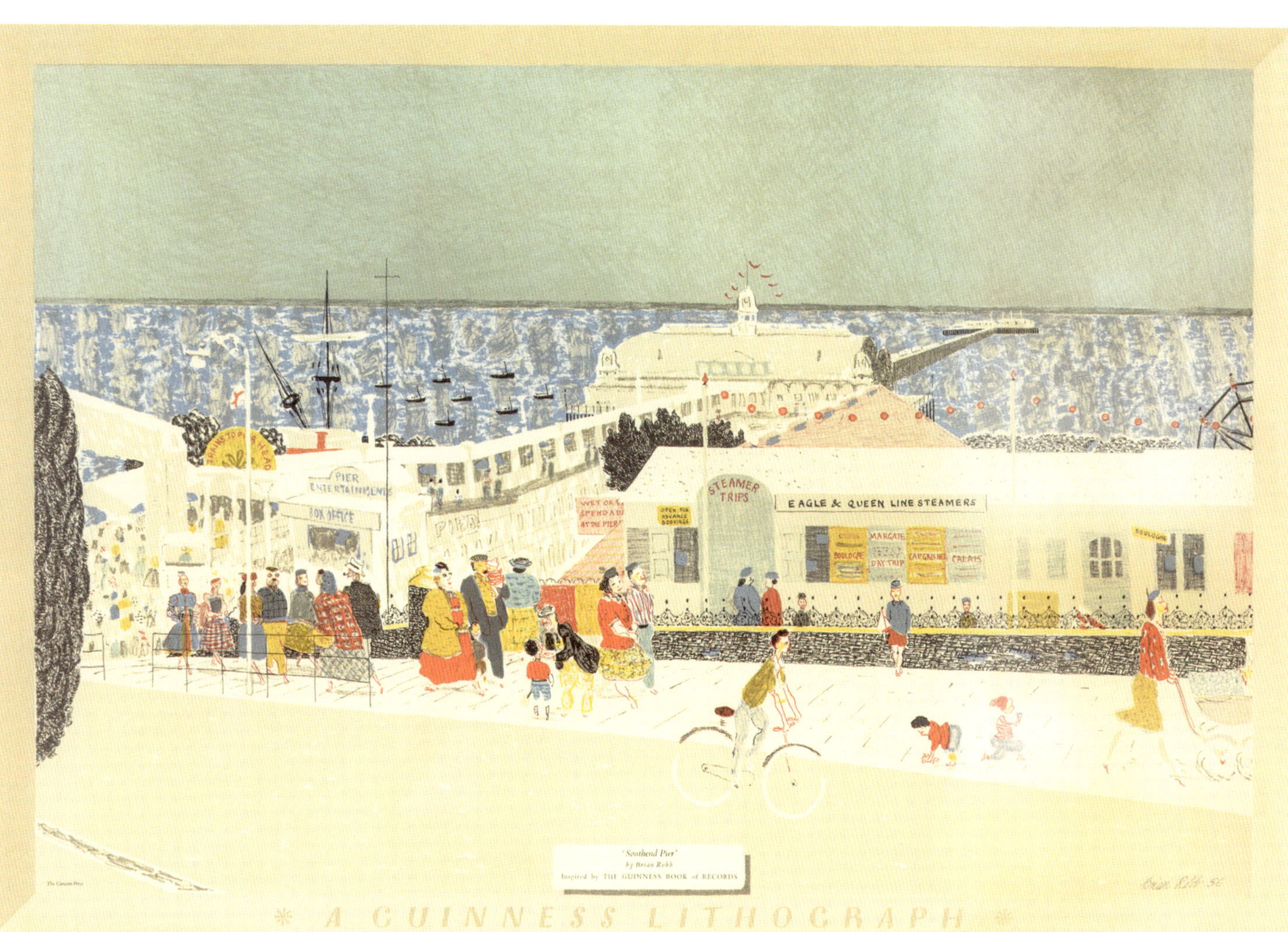

'Southend Pier'
by Brian Robb
Inspired by THE GUINNESS BOOK of RECORDS

The Curwen Press

A GUINNESS LITHOGRAPH

* A GUINNESS LITHOGRAPH *

The Guinness Lithographs
Second Series
1962

Doggett's Coat and Badge

Lithograph, image size 38cm x 50cm

David Gentleman (b.1930)

Gentleman chose the record for the earliest rowing race in the section on Rowing in the Sport chapter. He illustrates the record for the world's oldest sculling race:

'The earliest established sculling race is the Doggett's Coat and Badge which was first rowed on 1st August 1715, on a course from London Bridge to Chelsea and is still being rowed every year over the same course, under the administration of the Fishmonger's company.'

The Guinness Book of Records 1955 p.184

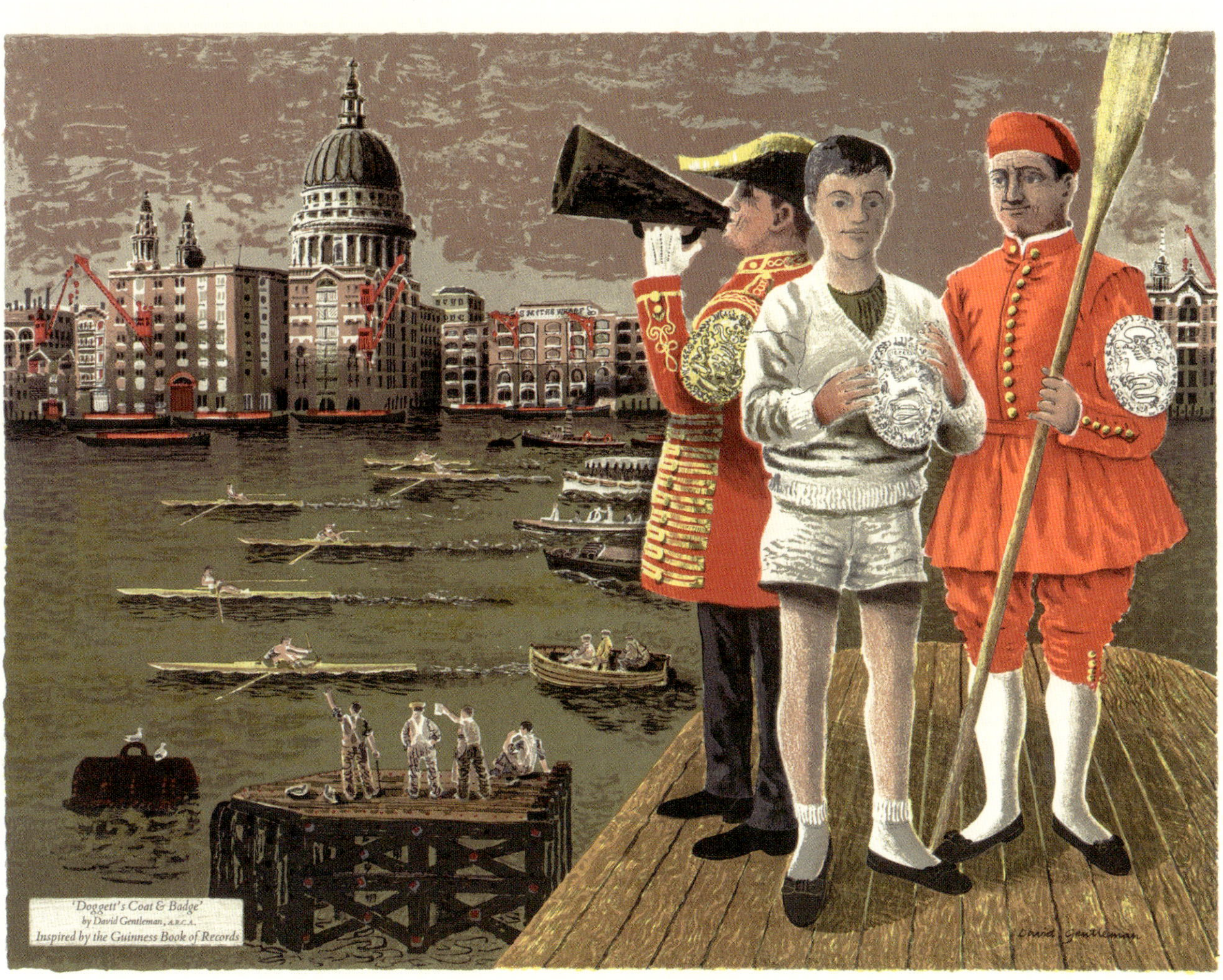

'Doggett's Coat & Badge'
by David Gentleman, A.R.C.A.
Inspired by the Guinness Book of Records

Pigeon Racing

Lithograph, image size 38cm x 50cm

Alistair Grant (1925-97)

Grant chose a subject relevant to pub audiences in the 1950s, Pigeon Racing, very popular at the time. This is in the section for Pigeon Racing in the Sport chapter. The world records are for the earliest reference to pigeon racing, the longest duration for a homing flight and the best speeds.

The Guinness Book of Records 1955 p.183

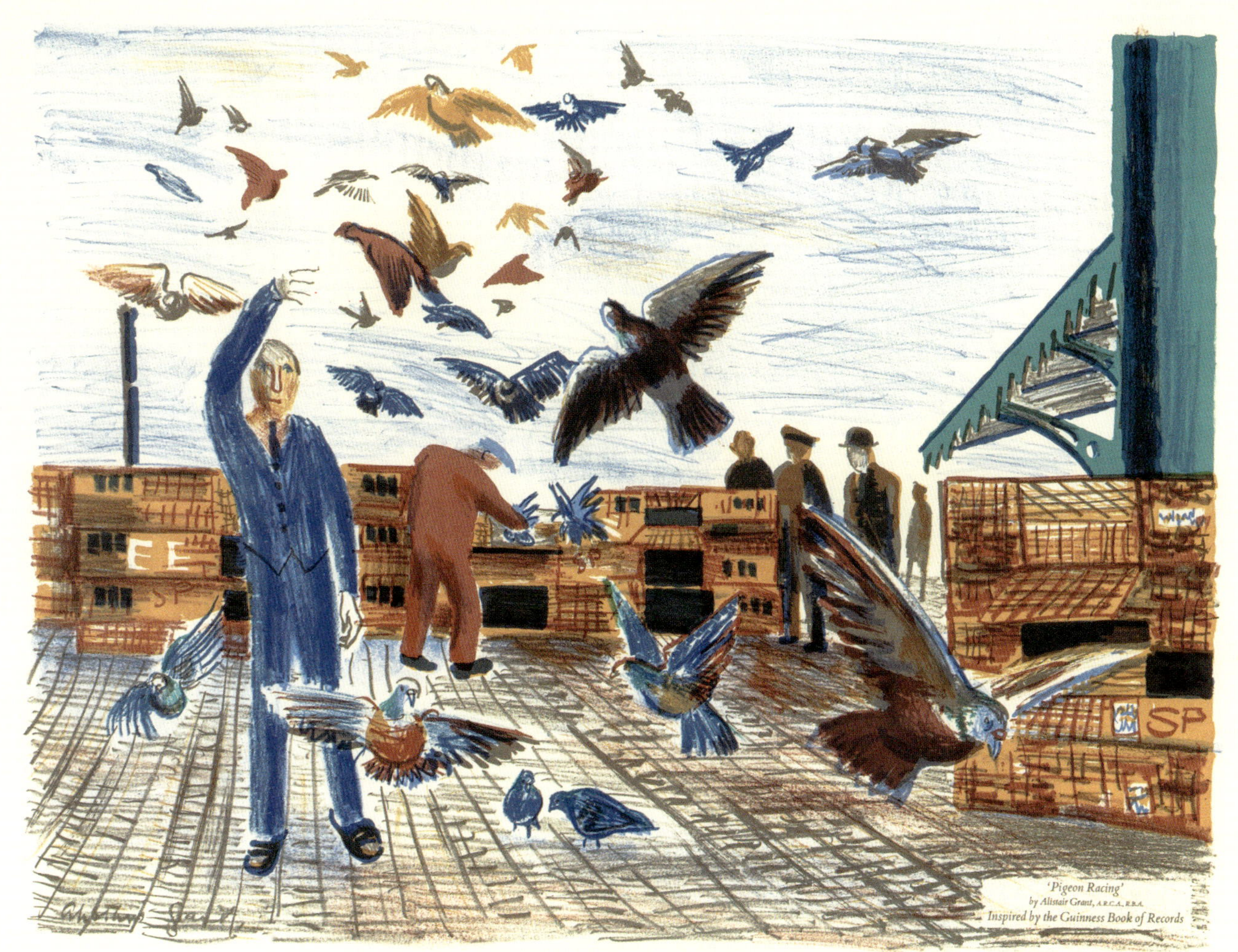

'Pigeon Racing'
by Alistair Grant, A.R.C.A., R.B.A.
Inspired by the Guinness Book of Records

Radcliffe Camera

Lithograph, image size 38cm x 50cm

Richard Guyatt (1914-2007)

Guyatt illustrates Radcliffe Camera in Oxford. Oxford is described as holding the record for the oldest university in Britain in the chapter The Human World in the section on Education:

'The oldest University in the British Isles is the University of Oxford which came into being c.1167.'

The Guinness Book of Records 1955 p.83

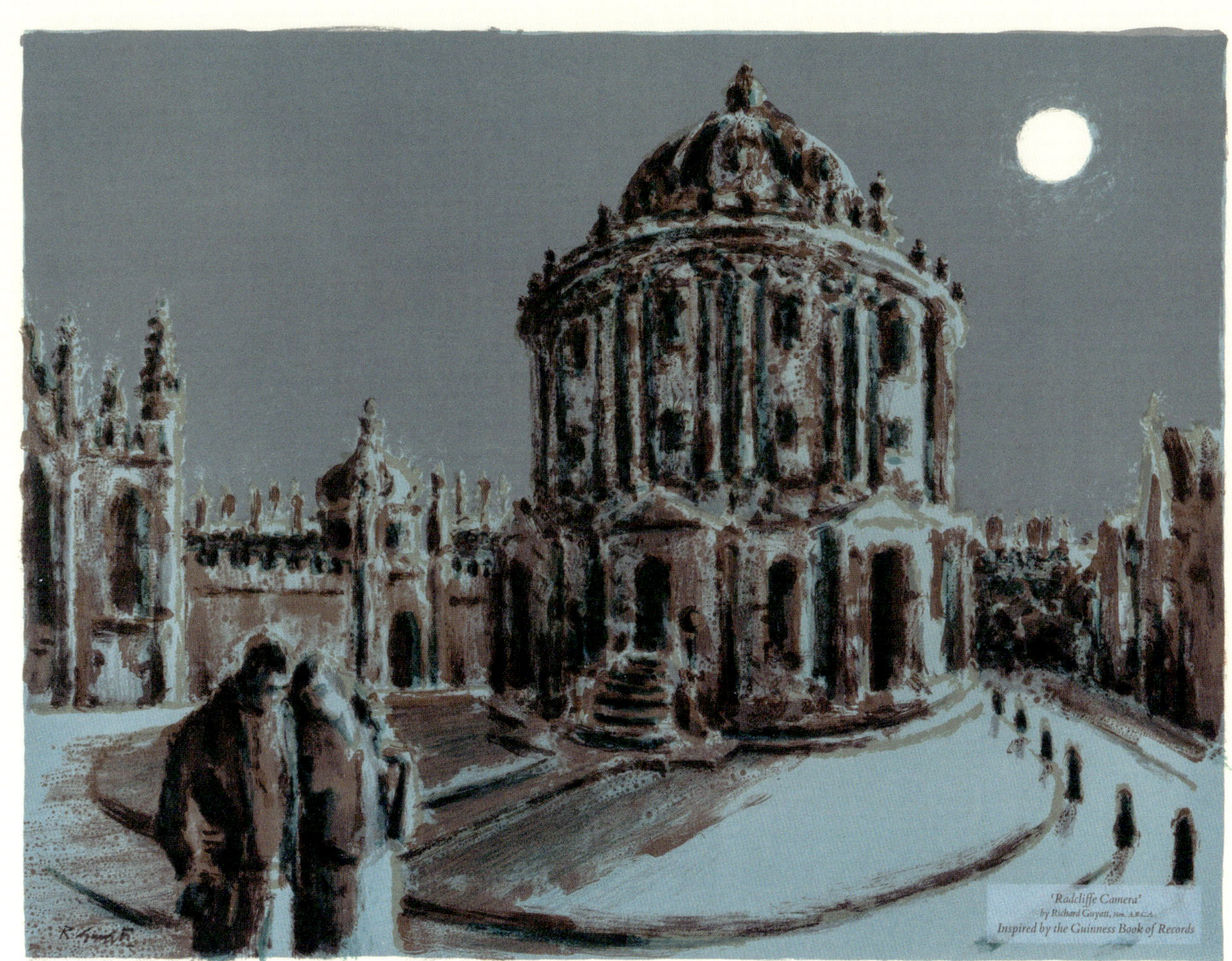

'Radcliffe Camera'
by Richard Guyatt, Hon. A.R.C.A.
Inspired by the Guinness Book of Records

Royal Albert Dock, London

Lithograph, image size 38cm x 50cm

Leonard Rosoman (1913-2012)

Rosoman illustrated a subject from the chapter The Human World. He illustrates Royal Albert Dock, which held the world record for being the busiest port:

'The largest and busiest dock complex in the world is that administered by the Port of London Authority. The five main dock systems which are run by the PLA cover an area of 4,410 acres of which 700 are water. In 1954 the Port handled a total of 53,793 ships.'

The Guinness Book of Records 1955 p.65

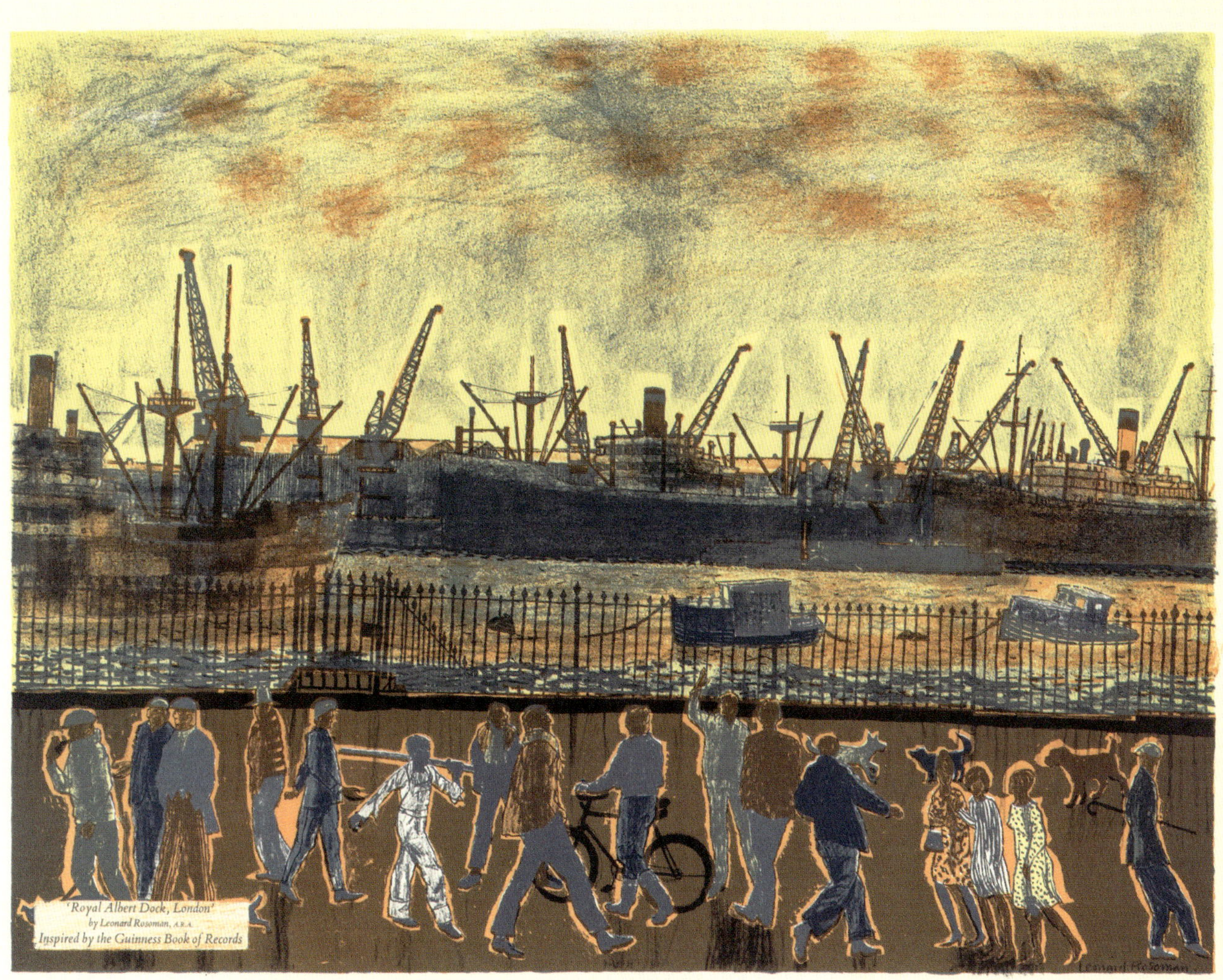

'Royal Albert Dock, London'
by Leonard Rosoman, A.R.A.
Inspired by the Guinness Book of Records

Sailing at Cork

Lithograph, image size 38cm x 50cm

Rosamund Steed (b.1937)

Steed chose a record from the Sport chapter in the section on Yachting. The image shows sailing at Cork, which held the world record as the oldest yacht club:

'The earliest club is the Royal Cork Yacht Club (formerly the Cork Harbour Water Club) established in Ireland in 1720.'

The Guinness Book of Records 1955 p.192

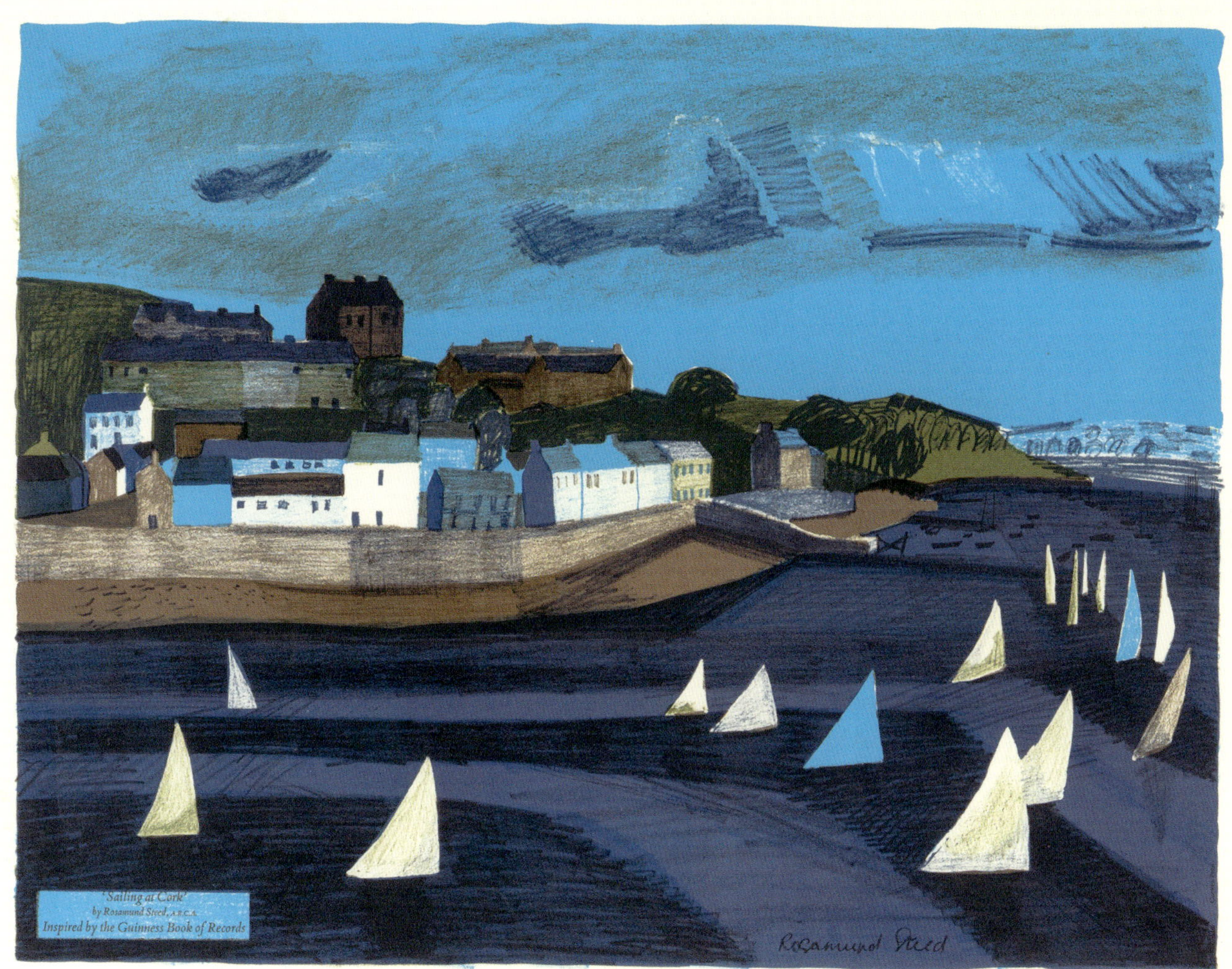

'Sailing at Cork'
by Rosamund Steed, A.R.C.A.
Inspired by the Guinness Book of Records
Rosamund Steed

Cup Tie

Lithograph, image size 38cm x 50cm

Carel Weight (1908-97)

Weight chose to illustrate an image relating to football, a very relevant subject for the audience and the discussions in the pubs. The section on Football in the Sport chapter is long and covers many records, highest scores, most caps, crowds.

The Guinness Book of Records 1955 p.167-169

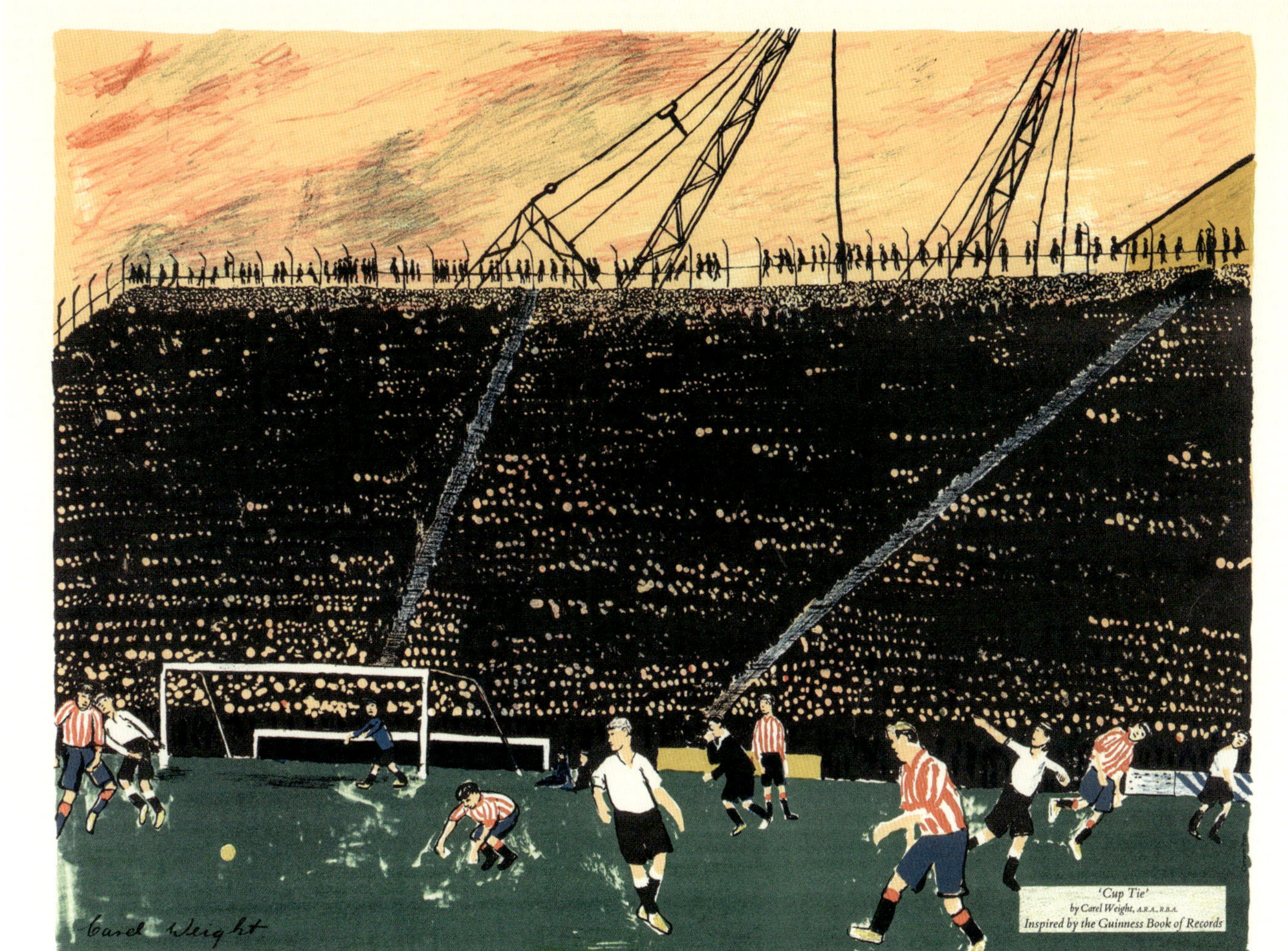

Carel Weight
'Cup Tie'
by Carel Weight, A.R.A., R.B.A.
Inspired by the Guinness Book of Records

The Artists

Edward Ardizzone

1900-79

Edward Ardizzone was born in 1900 in Haiphong in French Indo-China to a Franco-Italian father and a Scottish mother. The family returned to England in 1905, and lived mainly in East Anglia until 1919, when they settled in London. Ardizzone was educated at Clayesmore School in the Thames Valley, and it was there that he first developed his artistic talent. His first job, aged nineteen, was as a statistical clerk and in the evenings he attended Westminster School of Art (1921-26) under Bernard Meninsky and Walter Bayes. This was his only formal art training. After seven years as a clerk, he decided to take up a career as a painter and illustrator, and began to exhibit in solo shows at the Bloomsbury (1930) and Leger Galleries (1931-36). This was soon followed by other exhibitions. He became known for his illustration work and his illustrated stories, the first of which was *Little Tim and the Brave Sea-Captain* (Oxford, 1936). In the war he was called up to join the Royal Artillery and in 1940 he was appointed as an Official War Artist, recording the German invasion of France and the North African and Italian campaigns. After the war he worked successfully as an artist and illustrator, holding many exhibitions. He taught illustration at Camberwell School of Art and etching at the Royal College of Art (1953-61). He was elected to the Royal Academy of Arts in 1970 and awarded a CBE in 1971. He continued to work until his death in 1979.

Bernard Cheese

1925-2013

Bernard Cheese was born in Sydenham in 1925 and he studied at Beckenham School of Art where Carel Weight was one of his tutors. After four years in the army during the Second World War he attended the Royal College of Art (1947-50). Here he studied under Edward Bawden, John Nash and Edwin La Dell. It was La Dell in particular who influenced Cheese in his use of lithography. Cheese made a mural for the interior of the Shot Tower for the 1951 Festival of Britain. Cheese married fellow student Sheila Robinson and they moved to Great Bardfield in Essex in the 1950s where they lived near other artists of the day such as Edward Bawden. Cheese taught printmaking at St Martin's School of Art (1950-68) and later he became Senior Lecturer at Goldsmith's College, London (1970-79). He also taught part-time at the Central School of Art and Crafts in London (1980-89). He continued to work on his own printmaking and illustration and had commissions from clients such as the BBC and A&C Black. Cheese was a founder member of The Printmakers Council and in 1998 he was elected an RE a Fellow of the Royal Society of Painter-Etchers.

Barnett Freedman
1901-58

Barnett Freedman was born in 1901 in the east end of London, the son of Jewish immigrants from Russia. Freedman's only formal education was at primary school as from the age of nine to thirteen he suffered from chronic asthma related ill health, and spent much time in hospital where he spent hours reading and drawing. Aged fifteen, Freedman's talent for drawing led to jobs as a draughtsman. After five years evening study at St Martin's School of Art, London, he won a scholarship to the Royal College of Art (1922-25). Following college he tried to earn a living as a painter and after a few difficult years gained an introduction to publishers Faber and Faber for whom he designed book jackets, auto-lithographed on stone with hand-drawn lettering. He went on to illustrate many books and also worked on packaging design. He is remembered chiefly as a pioneer of colour auto-lithography for machine production at the Curwen and Baynard presses. He had a leading role in the production of large-scale colour prints for Contemporary Lithographs (1937), Lyons (1947, 1951, 1955) and Guinness (1956). In 1932, he was appointed instructor of still life at the Royal College of Art and shortly after also taught at the Ruskin School of Drawing in Oxford. At the outbreak of the Second World War he was appointed an official war artist with the British Expeditionary Force in France, then with the Admiralty. His work as war artist included large-scale paintings, portraits of entire ships' crews and the notable lithograph *15-inch Gun Turret in HMS Repulse*. Freedman was awarded a CBE for his work. He died at his studio in 1958.

David Gentleman

b.1930

David Gentleman was born in London in 1930 and grew up in Hertford. He studied at St Albans Art School, (1947-48) and following National Service as an education sergeant in the Royal Army Education Corps, he returned to art school in St Albans again in 1950. He then gained a place to study under Edward Bawden and John Nash at the Royal College of Art (1950-53), and was a tutor there for the following two years. From 1955 he worked as a freelance artist, illustrating and designing for many publishers and organisations. He designed postage stamps for the Royal Mail and coins for the Royal Mint, and in 1979 designed the murals for Charing Cross tube station. He also made wood engravings, lithographs and screen prints; posters for London Transport, the National Trust and placards for Stop the War Campaign (2003); logos and corporate identity for British Steel, logos for the National Trust, the Bodleian Library and publishers Duckworth and the Bodley Head. He has also illustrated many books and designed book jackets for Faber and Penguin, including the New Penguin Shakespeare series (1968-78). Gentleman has lived and worked in London and in Suffolk since 1956, and his travels around Britain and abroad have resulted in a series of highly successful publications, which include *David Gentleman's Britain* (1982) and its companion books on London, the British Coastline, Paris, India and Italy.

Ronald Glendening

1926-2013

Ronald Glendening was born in London in 1926. His father was a decorator but also made dolls houses and forts for toy soldiers. Glen, as he was known, showed artistic talent from a young age but his education was cut short by the war when, aged thirteen, he was evacuated to the east midlands. He never returned to school and by age fifteen he was back in London working as a messenger boy. When he was sixteen he enrolled at night school to study art at St Martin's School of Art (1949-51). He was awarded a scholarship to study graphic design at the Royal College of Art (1951-54) where his tutors included Edwin La Dell, John Nash, Edward Ardizzone and Edward Bawden. He paid for his studies by working as a station porter at Paddington and Kings' Cross stations. After college he worked on commissions for Shell, ICI, London Transport and Guinness. He also worked part-time as a teacher in lithography, etching and painting at Bromley, Camberwell and Croydon Colleges of Art and later he was employed as a court illustrator. In the 1970s and 80s he worked on animated graphics for London Weekend Television current affairs programmes. He enjoyed the company of other artists and was a frequent visitor to The French House and The Colony Rooms in London where his friends included artists such as Francis Bacon. He continued to paint and work in his studio in his home in North London until he died in 2013.

Alistair Grant

1925-97

Alistair Grant was born in 1925 in London. He grew up in the small fishing port of Etaples in Normandy, France, which was his mother's hometown and where he kept a house throughout his life. He studied at Birmingham College of Art (1941-43). After serving in Egypt with the Royal Air Force during the war, Grant returned to art school to study painting at the Royal College of Art (1947-50), where his tutors included Carel Weight and Ruskin Spear. Attracted to printmaking, he also studied lithography with Edwin La Dell and etching with Robert Austin. He was to remain closely associated with printmaking all his life. In the early 1950s he taught art in London at St Martin's School of Art and Hammersmith School of Art and also in Essex at Colchester School of Art. He became tutor in the printmaking department at the Royal College of Art (1955-70). Following Edwin La Dell's death in 1970 Grant became Head of the Printmaking department at the RCA where he continued to work until he retired in 1990 when he became Professor Emeritus at the RCA. He continued to paint and print, working in London and in Etaples, France until he died in London in 1997.

Richard Guyatt

1914-2007

Richard Guyatt was born in La Coruna in Galicia in North-West Spain. His father, who was the British Council in Vigo, died when Guyatt was ten at which time he was sent to school at Charterhouse in England. His talent as an artist was recognised and by age nineteen he was working as a freelance graphic designer working for Shell and BP as well as designing book illustrations. During the Second World War Guyatt worked in the camouflage unit. After the war he continued to work very successfully and co-designed the Lion and Unicorn Pavilion in the 1951 Festival of Britain. He designed stamps, coins, packaging and ceramics and was consultant designer to Wedgwood, which included making commemorative designs. Alongside his commercial career he taught at the Royal College of Art where he was Professor of Graphic Design (1948-78). At the RCA he set up a new school of Graphic Design with the aim to bring the teaching of design up to date and make it effective for British industry and commerce. With his energy, creativity and vision the graphic design department at the RCA became increasingly successful and gave graphic design and designers a new status. He was awarded a CBE in 1969 and continued to work until shortly before he died in 2007, aged ninety-one.

Edwin La Dell

1914-70

Thomas Edwin La Dell was born in Rotherham, Yorkshire. He attended Sheffield School of Art (1930-34). In 1935 he won a scholarship to the Royal College of Art (RCA) studying under John Nash, Percy Horton, Gilbert Spencer and Charles Mahoney. He studied etching under Robert Austin. La Dell was appointed as an official war artist during the Second World War, working on both public murals and camouflage. He later taught lithography at the Royal College of Art from 1948, becoming Head of the School of Engraving and Etching from 1950 where he continued to work until he died in 1970. He established a major lithographic studio at the RCA and was acknowledged as one of the leading lithographers of the time. He exhibited widely and published his own prints in addition to illustrating books for Faber & Faber and the Folio Society. La Dell created lithographs for The School Prints scheme and for Lyons Tea Rooms Series. He also instigated The Coronation Series of Lithographs at the RCA in 1953 and then a few years later the Wapping to Windsor Series in 1960.

Brian Robb

1913-79

Brian Robb was born in Scarborough in 1913. He went to school at Malvern College and later studied at Chelsea College of Art (1930-34). He then studied at the Slade School of Art (1935-36). He was a very accomplished painter and illustrator and his early career involved work as a cartoonist for the magazine *Punch*. He also worked as an illustrator designing posters and press advertisements for Shell and also London Transport. He also wrote and illustrated children's books. He worked as a lecturer at Chelsea School of Art (1936-62), with a break for service during the Second World War when he was a Lieutenant in the Camouflage Unit building dummy tanks in the Middle East. During the latter part of his career he taught at the Royal College of Art (1961-78), becoming Professor of Illustration until he retired in 1978.

Leonard Rosoman

1913-2012

Leonard Rosoman was born 27 October 1913 in Hampstead, London and was educated at Deacons School, Peterborough. He studied at King Edward VII School of Art, Durham University (1930-34), at the Royal Academy Schools (1935-36) and at the Central School of Arts and Crafts (1937-38) under Bernard Meninsky. As a student he was influenced by Gauguin, Paul Nash and Edward Burra. He taught painting at the Reimann School, Westminster, (1938-39). During the war he served in the National Fire Service in London and in 1944 he was appointed Official War Artist to the Admiralty. His work from this period was exhibited much later, in 1989, in *A War Retrospective* at the Imperial War Museum. After the war he continued to work as a painter, illustrator and designer. His first one-man exhibition was held at the St George's Gallery 1946. He taught illustration at Camberwell School of Arts and Crafts (1947-48) and mural painting at Edinburgh College of Art (1948-56). While there he made drawings for the Radio Times and produced his first significant mural for the Festival of Britain in 1951 and a later mural for the 1958 British Pavilion at the Brussels World Fair. In 1956, he became a tutor in the Painting School of the Royal College Of Art (1956-78) with Peter Blake and David Hockney among his students. He was elected an associate of the Royal Academy in 1960, and a full academician a decade later. He was awarded an OBE in 1981.

Rosamund Steed

b.1937

Rosamund Steed was born in Ipswich in 1937. She studied at St Martin's School of Art where one of her tutors was Bernard Cheese. It was Cheese who encouraged her to apply to the Royal College of Art, which she did, and she took a place to study there from 1958-61. She studied printmaking under tutors Julian Trevelyan and Edwin La Dell and sculpture under tutors Elizabeth Frink and Robert Clatworthy. In the 1970s she returned to live in the East of England, in Suffolk where she ran her own etching workshop. She also taught at Gainsborough House in Sudbury and was an early member of the Gainsborough House Print Workshop. Rosamund married her husband Ronald Harry Fuller in 1962, and works under the name of Moss Fuller.

Carel Weight

1908-97

Carel Weight was born in London in 1908. Weight studied at Hammersmith School of Art (1928-30) where he met the artist Ruskin Spear. Weight chose to leave Hammersmith School in 1931 and continued his studies at Goldsmiths College, London. In the same year his work was shown in the Summer Exhibition at the Royal Academy, where he regularly exhibited his paintings throughout his career. He taught at Beckenham School of Art (1932-42) and had his first solo exhibition at Cooling Galleries, London in 1934. During the Second World War Weight was called up to the Royal Engineers and taught with the Army Education Corps before being employed as an Official War Artist. After the war Weight taught at the Royal College of Art, where he became Professor of Painting. He was awarded a CBE in 1962 and elected RA in 1965. A retrospective exhibition was held at the Royal Academy in 1982, and an exhibition was held at Hastings Museum and Art Gallery in 1988 to celebrate his eightieth birthday. He was appointed Companion of Honour in 1995, and died two years later in London.

References

1. Norris McWhirter, 'The Story Behind the Guinness Book of Records', *Guinness Time*, Christmas issue 1955.

2. 'Who, Where, When, How Many?' *Guinness Time*, Christmas issue 1962.

3. Rt Hon The Earl of Iveagh 'Foreword', *The Guinness Book of World Records*, September 1955.

4. TL Marks, Letter to artists, 9th April 1955.

5. 'TL Marks. A man of imagination and understanding' *Guinness Time* Autumn issue 1971.

6. Charlie Batchelor, *Tea and a Slice of Art. The Lyons Lithographs 1946-55*, p30.

7. TL Marks, Letter to Barnett Freedman, November 1955.

8. TL Marks, Letter to Barnett Freedman, November 1955.

9. Charlie Batchelor, *Tea and a Slice of Art. The Lyons Lithographs 1946-55*, p18.

10 . Pat Gilmour, 'Postwar Printmaking and the Curwen Studio' *Artists at Curwen*, The Tate Gallery 1977, p95.

11. Ruth Artmonsky, *Art For Everyone Contemporary Lithographs Ltd*, Artmonsky Arts p18.

12. TL Marks, Letter to Barnett Freedman, 15th March 1956.

13. TL Marks, Letter to Barnett Freedman, April 1956.

14. TL Marks, Letter to Barnett Freedman and artists, April 1956.

15. Barnett Freedman, 'Autolithography or Substitue Works of Art' *Penrose Annual*, Vol 44, 1950.

16. Simon Lawrence, *Barnett Freedman The Graphic Art*, The Fleece Press, p99.

Emma Mason opened Emma Mason Prints in 2004. The gallery specialises in original prints by artists working in Britain from the post-war years to the present day. Emma studied Art History and Italian at Leicester University. After many years working in the fruit trade as an importer Emma changed career to set up the gallery. Emma has written about post-war original prints for various publications and, with her husband Richard, has published two books on the printmaker Robert Tavener.

www.emmamason.co.uk